PLANT-BASED
BOOT CAMP

VEGAN FOOD FOR PEOPLE WHO DON'T LIKE VEGAN FOOD

BY MICHAEL NOLAN

Plant-Based Boot Camp acknowledges the artistry of the following font designers, whose hard work makes this book look so awesome:

Alegreya Font by Juan Pablo del Peral
ALPHA ECHO Font by Vic Fieger
Diavlo Font by Jos Buivenga
Handlee Font by Joe Prince

ISBN-13: 978-0-692-82340-8
Published by Fios and Fado Press

www.plantbasedbootcamp.com

CONTENTS

ROASTED CHICKPEAS

PAGE 111

To Darin, for inspiring me to return to a plant-based diet and for dealing with me while I wrote about it,

To my Kickstarter supporters, without whom this book would not exist, and

To those who are brave enough to seek a change in their diets,

...this is for you.

INTRODUCTION

When I decided to become vegetarian as a teen in the Southern U.S., I did so without the support of my family. In fact, my stepmother was so strangely invested in my failure, she would routinely cook entire meals in which every item contained some sort of meat. As a result, I ate a lot of bread and crackers. Back then, I'd think nothing of making a meal of candy though, so my palate was as decidedly juvenile as I was.

Over the years, I changed and so did my diet. A lot of years passed, with a lot of travel and time spent living in cities known for incredible food. As an adult, my passion for food – and my meager income – led me to teach myself to cook. In turn, I wanted to help others learn to cook, as was my goal when I wrote *Food Camp* in March of 2014. Months later, I made the transition back to a plant-based diet. This time, though, I had the tools I needed to prepare delicious meals that rival many restaurants, with the added benefit of being entirely plant-based.

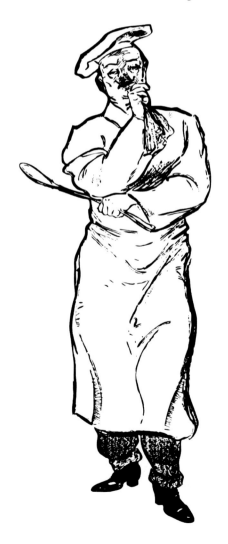

After years of crafting my own recipes, I could now challenge myself to improve on them by making them healthier, cheaper, *and* completely free of meat, dairy, and animal products. That personal challenge, along with the sheer number of friends and readers asking for my recipes, led to the creation of this book. Inspired by my own experience, and three years of hard work, this collection is a step-by-step instructional guide that makes it possible for virtually anyone to enjoy a plant-based diet without feeling like they are going without.

I'm not one of the folks who will yell and scream until you give up your beloved meat and cheese; that's neither my responsibility nor my business. My only goal with this book is to create the tools that enable you to make informed decisions based on firsthand knowledge. You will learn to prepare new foods, and you'll make old favorites in surprising new ways.

Perhaps you are struggling with that voice in your head (or on social media) reminding you that you are a carnivore. *How could you even think about living without bacon?* I'm not here to preach, and I'm not telling you to give up what you love. I only want to present you with healthy and delicious options. The beauty of this life is that we all have the gift of choice; we can become a new-and-improved version of ourselves whenever we choose.

Choose well.

FAQ

Anyone who chooses a particular diet that falls outside of the mainstream is bound to get questions, and plant-based eaters get a lot of them. In this section I share answers to a few of the more important ones.

Why go plant-based?

There are three primary reasons behind the choice to eat a plant-based diet: personal health, animal rights, and environmental stewardship:

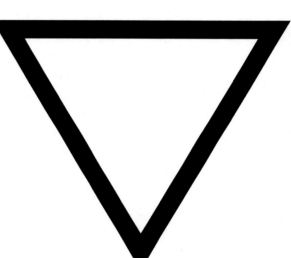

HEALTH

A plant-based diet can help to quickly reverse conditions like Type 2 diabetes, high blood pressure, cardiovascular disease, and high cholesterol, while making it easier to control your weight. That's not to say that everyone who eats a vegan diet is healthy.

ANIMAL RIGHTS

I'm not going to go in-depth on the topic here, because a book that focuses on food shouldn't make you throw up before you start cooking. I will say that the factory farming industry is pretty vile, and the way they treat animals is, by and large, worse than a horror flick.

ENVIRONMENTAL STEWARDSHIP

Did you know that it takes about 2,500 gallons of water to produce a single pound of beef? I'm not going to get on a soap box here either, but there are plenty of statistics out there, and quite a few documentaries that are worth your time.

While each reason is entirely valid on its own, you might find that you have more than one. I like to think of it as a pyramid, and it's up to each of us to decide where we place ourselves on it. It is also important to accept that not everyone will agree with us, and that we all come with our own sets of values. We learn in different ways and have different life experiences that inform our decisions.

Can a 100% plant-based diet be healthy?

The simple answer is yes. That said, there are a lot of unhealthy vegetarians and vegans out there. Just removing animal products from your diet is not going to automatically make you healthy. A plant-based diet can be completely healthy and provide you with all of the calories and nutrition you need to live a healthy, vibrant lifestyle, but you need to pay attention to what, how, and when you are eating.

I strongly encourage you to limit the overall amount of processed food you eat. In my experience, it helps to think about it in reverse. Instead of thinking about the things you shouldn't eat, think about all of the good stuff you get to enjoy. For example, I'm totally allowed to have that ice cream at the end of the day, provided I have already eaten all of the fresh fruit and vegetables required to meet my nutritional needs for that day. If I've eaten more than my share of processed foods, I try to replace those snacks with more nutrient-rich fresh fruit.

If I want to eat that doughnut in the morning (and I really do), I know I need to increase my exercise that day to burn off the extra 200 calories of deliciousness. An hour of walking at a steady pace can burn about 300 calories (that's 1 ½ doughnuts), by the way.

But what about protein?

This is the number one question that plant-based eaters get, and the first excuse people will offer for not wanting to try a plant-based diet. We have become a protein-focused society, when the truth is that we need far less than most think. Did you know that the human body can't store excess protein, and that it strains the liver and kidneys to eliminate what we don't need? That being said, there are plenty of plant-based protein sources to be found. As a general rule, we need roughly .36 grams of protein for every pound of body weight. A man weighing 160 pounds, for example, should have about 57 grams of protein per day. Here are some of my favorite protein sources:

ALMONDS	**CHIA SEEDS**	**LENTILS**
ARUGULA	**CHICKPEAS**	**OATMEAL**
BROWN RICE	**GRAPEFRUIT**	**QUINOA**
BLACK BEANS	**HEMP SEED**	**ZUCCHINI**

While some protein sources are better than others, even a grapefruit contains nearly 1.5 grams of protein. Eat a well-balanced diet that consists primarily of whole, plant-based foods, and you are going to get the protein you need.

Where do you get your calcium?

Most men under 70 and women under 50 need 1000 mg of calcium per day. People over those age groups should get about 1200 mg. Typical diets are highly acidic, which explains why so many people are popping acid reducers like candy these days. That's not news to you, I'm sure. What you may not know is that when your body becomes too acidic, it will do whatever it can to lower the acid level, including leeching calcium from tissue and bone.

Dairy milk is high in calcium, right? Yes, it is. But processed dairy is acidic. Higher levels of phosphorus mean that our bodies don't absorb the calcium nearly as well as the industry might have us believe. So how do plant-based eaters do it?

Here are some of my favorite sources of calcium:

CHIA SEEDS	**HEMP MILK**	**SPINACH**
CHICKPEAS	**KALE**	**SOYBEANS**
COLLARDS	**MOLASSES**	**TAHINI**
FIGS	**NAVY BEANS**	**TURNIP GREENS**

Want to meet your daily need for calcium in a single, delicious meal? Make a breakfast with oatmeal using hemp milk, and add almonds, chia, molasses, and maple syrup. That's it. Enjoy your breakfast and go about your day without worrying about calcium.

Where do you get your B12?

Vitamin B12 can be a tough nut to crack. It's only found in plant-based foods when those sources have been fortified. Fortified plant-based foods use certain bacteria as their source material, and you can find B12 fortified versions of everything from meat replacements to milks and cereals. Both Bragg® and Red Star® brands offer fortified nutritional yeast that provide a lot of B12. There are a lot of recipes in this book that use nutritional yeast, so get some! 1 1/2 tablespoons of fortified B12 gives you what you need for the day, and it tastes great.

That said, getting the recommended amount of B12 in your daily diet will be a challenge, so if you eat a 100% plant-based diet, I recommend taking a vegan-friendly supplement.

What about iron?

Okay, ladies. I'm going to talk to you for a minute because this is one area where I'm pretty sure you're failing your body. Men only need about 8 mg of iron per day, while women between the ages of 19 and 50 need more than twice that amount – roughly 18 mg!

Dark chocolate is not only enticingly delicious, it's packed with iron. A three ounce portion provides 10 mg! Beans and legumes are surprisingly good sources of iron as well. Other sources include:

CASHEWS	**KIDNEY BEANS**	**SPINACH**
CHARD	**MOLASSES**	**SPIRULINA**
DARK CHOCOLATE	**RAISINS**	**TOFU**
LENTILS	**SESAME SEEDS**	**QUINOA**

How do I deal with peer pressure to eat meat?

Peer pressure has been in our lives for as long as we've been social creatures, and the peer pressure that would try to coerce you to eat meat, dairy, or anything else you have expressed a desire to avoid is no different from the peer pressure that would try to talk you into doing anything else you don't want to do. In my own experience, I learned that the peer pressure only bothered me as long as I gave it the permission to.

I find that the pressure to eat animal products comes from one of two places. Either you are struggling with a need to fit in with your peer group, or you are struggling with your decision to avoid animal products, or both. Focus your attention on dealing with those issues, and the peer pressure will all but disappear.

I want to try, but where do I start?

A full overhaul of your diet can be scary, because it's a big change. Don't get overwhelmed by trying to to everything at once, or you're more likely to become frustrated and give up completely.

Start with one meal. Find one completely plant-based food that you can make and enjoy, and add that to your weekly routine. Just like that, you've replaced one meal per week. Then add another. And another. In no time, you'll be eating fewer animal products and you won't miss them. Just take it at your own pace and make sure that you are enjoying what you're eating. Life's too short to eat crappy food.

DRINKS

BANANABERRY
BLAST

PAGE 9

NUT MILK
PAGE 8

LEMONADE
PAGE 11

THE BIG
GREEN

PAGE 10

NUT MILKS

Alternative milks can be every bit as useful and delicious as dairy milk, and they're not just for vegans. There are lots of people who live with lactose intolerance, so having an alternative means they don't have to give up all of their favorite foods. Nut milks are a relatively quick and easy option to make at home, and you don't need a lot of special equipment or a lot of time to make it happen. I do recommend that you invest in a nut milk bag, but they are easily found for around five dollars, so they won't break the bank.

> 1 cup almonds, cashews, or pecans
> 4 cups water
> ¼ teaspoon salt
> sweetener of choice (optional)

1. Soak the nuts in enough water to cover them by 1", for at least 12 hours. The long soak time makes the milk creamier.

2. Drain the soaked nuts and transfer to a blender along with 4 cups of water.

3. Blend on high speed for three minutes.

4. Strain the milk through a nut milk bag or fine mesh strainer and sweeten if desired.

Don't get rid of the stuff that's left in the bag! That's nut meal, and it can be used as a nutritious add-in for smoothies, baked goods or granola, or dehydrate it to make nut flour (which isn't cheap, by the way).

SMOOTHIES

Smoothies are a popular meal-replacing beverage for several reasons. For starters, they're pretty darn delicious, not to mention how packed they are with nutrition. Even better, they take very little time to make.

These are just a few of the many smoothie recipes I've come up with over the years, but truth be told, I almost never follow a recipe. You can make a smoothie out of just about any combination of fresh and frozen fruits, juices, milks, and leafy greens. Try these out, then start using what you have on hand to come up with your own masterpieces.

BANANABERRY BLAST

2 frozen bananas
a spoonful of coconut oil
6-8 frozen strawberries
1/2 cup blueberries
a handful of fresh baby spinach

MANGO AVOCADO

1 ripe avocado
2 cups frozen mango
1 cup coconut water
1/2 cup orange juice

BANANA NUT MUFFIN

2 frozen bananas
2 tablespoons nut butter
2 cups milk
1 cup ice

PEACH PIE

2 cups frozen peach slices
1 cup milk
a small handful of nuts
a splash of vanilla extract
2 pitted dates
1/2 teaspoon cinnamon

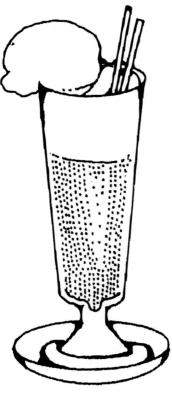

THE BIG GREEN

2 handfuls fresh spinach
2 cups water or milk
3 cups frozen fruit chunks

GREEN SLIME (KID APPROVED!)

1 medium avocado
1/2 cup milk
4 teaspoons maple syrup
4 teaspoons lime juice
1 teaspoon lime zest
1/4 teaspoon salt

Now that I've given you some basic recipes to play with, I'm going to offer a few quick tips to make your smoothie making life even easier:

1. Buy fruit when it is on sale and save yourself a ton of time and effort by cutting it up and prepping it in freezer-safe containers ahead of time. Bonus points because frozen fruit can often take the place of adding ice to a smoothie.

2. Always have peeled, cut up, frozen bananas on hand. They make for the creamiest smoothies ever.

3. Smoothies are a great way to incorporate extra veggies into your diet, if that's an issue for you. Spinach in a smoothie will definitely change the way it looks, but in most drinks it doesn't really change the flavor much at all.

LEMONADE

      1 cup sugar
      1 cup fresh lemon juice
      2 quarts water

I'm going to assume you can figure out how to combine sugar, lemon juice, and water in a pitcher, but I will tell you that using room temperature or even slightly warm water will make it easier to dissolve the sugar. Then, refrigerate until chilled or pour over ice.

You can also get fancy and make limeade using the same recipe, by replacing the lemon juice for lime juice. Or go halfsies, if that's your thing. Do you, cupcake.

MASALA CHAI

      3 cups water
      6 black peppercorns
      4 cardamom pods
      3 star anise
      2 cinnamon sticks, broken into pieces
      4 whole cloves
      1" piece of fresh ginger
      2 tablespoons sugar (to taste)
      3 tablespoons black tea (or 3 tea bags)
      3 cups milk

1. In a large pot, bring water to boil. Add the peppercorns, cardamom, star anise, cinnamon, cloves, and ginger.

2. Boil for 5 minutes and reduce heat to low.

3. Add tea and sugar and simmer for 3 minutes.

4. Add soy milk. Let simmer for another 2 minutes.

5. Remove from heat and strain.

MULLED CIDER

      8 cups (1/2 gallon) apple cider
      2-4 cinnamon sticks
      2-4 whole dried cloves
      2 whole allspice berries (optional)
      2 cardamom pods
      1 orange or apple, sliced thinly horizontally (optional)
      brown sugar, agave nectar, or maple syrup to taste (optional)

1. Add ingredients to a slow cooker and simmer for several hours on low.

2. Alternatively, bring cider to a slow boil on the stove and add remaining ingredients. Reduce heat to low and simmer for 30 minutes.

KOMBUCHA

The key ingredient for making kombucha is called a SCOBY, i.e. what makes the fermentation magic happen. While it is possible to make a SCOBY from scratch, it's a lot more complicated than we have time for here, so I'll suggest that you either source a SCOBY from a friend, or order one from Etsy like I did.

Once you have a SCOBY, all you need to make your first batch of kombucha is a large wide-mouth container (mine is 1-gallon), some tea, some sugar, and a little distilled vinegar.

IMPORTANT NOTE: If you are making kombucha at home and see any mold whatsoever, you should discard the tea and the SCOBY, as it is no longer safe to consume.

Start by boiling 3 1/2 quarts of water, turning off the heat and adding 6 regular tea bags. Let the tea steep for 20 minutes then remove the bags and stir in 2 cups of sugar. Leave the tea to cool completely to room temperature before moving on to the next step. Clean and sterilize a large mouth gallon jar in the dishwasher, making sure to never use antibacterial soap. Then add your SCOBY and about a cup of kombucha from the previous batch, if available. If not, add ¼ cup of plain vinegar. When the tea has cooled, I add it to the jar and stir it for about 20 seconds.

Then, all that's left to do is cover the jar with a napkin and set it in a warm-ish, dark place for a few days. Seriously, that's it. Taste your kombucha with a straw periodically to figure out when the flavor is right for you. My magic number is 13 days.

BLOOD MARY MIX

When it comes to a Bloody Mary, it's all about the mix. Instead of buying a bottle, let's start by making some fresh juice. If you have a juicer, that's the quickest, easiest way to get where we're going. Just juice the following:

> 2 pounds tomatoes
> 2 celery stalks
> 3 garlic cloves, peeled
> 1 jalapeño pepper
> 1 carrot
> ½ medium Vidalia onion
> small handful fresh parsley
> 1 lemon, peeled

NOTE: No juicer? Just purée all of the ingredients in a food processor or high powered blender until smooth, then pour the mixture through a fine mesh strainer to remove the pulp.

To complete the mixer, stir in:

> 1 teaspoon sea salt
> 1-2 teaspoons fresh cracked black pepper
> 2 tablespoons soy sauce
> 1 tablespoon prepared horseradish

For the perfect Bloody Mary: fill a tall glass with ice, add 1 ounce of vodka, and fill with Mary mix. Top with a few dashes of your favorite hot sauce and garnish generously with a celery stick, carrot stick, olives, a lemon wedge, or whatever else strikes your fancy.

This Mary mix will keep in the fridge for a few days, if it lasts that long. If you run out of vodka, it's a pretty tasty veggie juice all by itself. But really, who runs out of vodka? I mean, don't invite me for brunch until you've restocked.

BREAKFAST

CREAMY GRITS

PAGE 18

COUNTRY
GRAVY

PAGE 103

EGGPLANT
BACON

PAGE 19

TOFU SCRAMBLE

1/2 block extra firm tofu (about 7 oz.)
1 teaspoon turmeric
1/2 teaspoon garlic powder
1/2 teaspoon onion powder
1/2 teaspoon salt
black pepper
cooking oil
2 cloves garlic, minced
1/2 medium sweet onion, chopped
1/2 sweet red pepper, chopped
Black Salt / Kala Namak (optional, for a more egg-like flavor)
pickled jalapeño slices (optional)

1. Drain tofu and wrap in a clean towel. Squeeze as much water as you can out, but don't get all OCD about it. Use your fingers or a fork to crumble the tofu into small pieces (to resemble scrambled eggs), and place in a bowl. Add turmeric, garlic powder, onion, powder, and salt, and toss to coat evenly.

2. Heat 2 tablespoons cooking oil in a large skillet over medium heat. Add vegetables and sauté for 4-5 minutes or until the onions are translucent and softened slightly.

3. Add tofu and cook for 5 minutes, stirring often, until the tofu is heated through.

HASH BROWNS

Russet potatoes
oil
salt & pepper
chopped onions (optional)

1. Shred the potatoes.

2. Pile shredded potatoes on a kitchen towel and roll it tightly to squeeze out as much of the moisture as you can. You want the potatoes to fry, not steam.

3. Heat oil in a skillet set to medium-high heat. When the oil is hot, add the potatoes.

4. Press the potatoes into a flat and even circle and cook for two minutes, or until the bottom is golden.

5. Flip and cook for two more minutes, until golden and crispy.

6. Season and drain on paper towels.

Don't be afraid to get creative here. If that all night waffle place can do it, you can too. Add onions, peppers, diced tomatoes, even vegan shreds. Heck, throw some leftover chili and pico on and dive right in.

PANCAKES & WAFFLES

    2 cups all-purpose flour
    1 tablespoon sugar
    2 tablespoons baking powder
    1/4 teaspoon salt
    1 1/2 cups milk (+/-)
    1/4 cup water
    1 tablespoon vinegar
    2 tablespoons aquafaba
    1 teaspoon vanilla
    cooking oil

1. Combine milk and vinegar in a small cup and stir, then set aside. Add flour, sugar, baking powder, starch, and salt to a mixing bowl and stir to thoroughly combine. Make a well in the center of the dry ingredients.

3. Pour the milk mixture into the center of the dry ingredients, followed by the water, aquafaba, and vanilla. With a large spoon or spatula, stir ingredients until just combined. Some lumps are okay.

4. For pancakes, pour about 1/4 cup at a time into a hot pan and cook over medium heat until the edges turn golden, then flip and cook until golden and done all the way through. For waffles, follow the guidelines on your wafflemaker.

FRENCH TOAST

1/2 tablespoon maple syrup
4 tablespoons aquafaba
1 cup milk
1/2 teaspoon cinnamon
1/2 teaspoon vanilla
4 slices bread
vegan butter

1. Mix ingredients up to bread in shallow bowl and set aside for a few minutes.

2. Heat a pan over medium and melt a little vegan butter.

3. One at a time, dip a slice of bread in the batter for a few seconds on each side.

4. Place in the pan and cook 2-3 minutes, or until the cooked side is golden brown. Flip and cook another 2 minutes, until both sides are golden.

CREAMY GRITS

1/2 cup cashews, soaked in water overnight
2 cups milk, divided
1/4 cup nutritional yeast
2 tablespoons oil
1/3 cup finely chopped white onion
1 teaspoon coarse sea salt, divided
3 cups vegan broth
3/4 cup yellow grits

1. Blend cashews, 1 cup milk, and nutritional yeast until smooth and set aside.

2. Sauté onion.

3. Meanwhile, bring 3 cups broth to a boil in a medium sauce pot. Add grits in a slow, but steady stream, whisking constantly, until mixture is smooth. When mixture comes to a boil, reduce heat to low.

4. Simmer grits, stirring occasionally, until most of the liquid has been absorbed.

5. Add 1 cup of milk and ½ teaspoon salt and cook, whisking constantly, until thickened, another 10 minutes.

6. Stir in cashew mixture and onions. Cover and cook, stirring occasionally, until grits are soft and fluffy, about 30 minutes.

EGGPLANT BACON

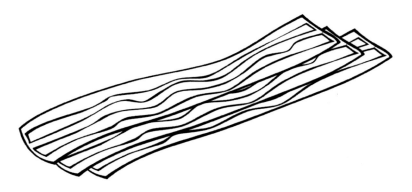

1 large eggplant (about 1 lb)
2 tablespoon apple cider vinegar
1 teaspoon liquid smoke
1 tablespoon soy sauce
2 tablespoons maple syrup
1 tablespoon olive oil
1/2 teaspoon garlic powder
1/2 teaspoon smoked paprika
1/2 teaspoon black pepper
1 teaspoon brown sugar (optional)

Preheat oven to 300F.

1. Cut the end from the eggplant and then cut it in half lengthwise. Use a mandoline slicer to thinly slice the eggplant into long strips. Cut the strips in half again lengthwise with a sharp knife.

2. Mix all remaining ingredients in a large zipper bag. Transfer the eggplant strips to the bag, seal, and toss to coat evenly. Lay the bag flat and allow the strips to marinate for 15 minutes.

4. Transfer strips to a baking sheet and bake for 30 minutes minutes, flipping the bacon after 15, so that it cooks evenly. Check for doneness (they should be fairly firm but not burnt) and continue to bake as needed, in five minute increments. The bacon will crisp when it cools.

BETTER THAN BUTTERMILK BISCUITS

4 tablespoons vegan butter
1 cup milk
1 tablespoon apple cider vinegar
2 cups all-purpose flour
1/2 teaspoon sea salt
1 tablespoon baking powder
1/2 teaspoon baking soda

Preheat oven to 450F.

1. Cut the vegan butter into small chunks and place in the freezer for 15 minutes.

2. In a small cup, combine milk and vinegar and set aside. This is vegan buttermilk!

3. In a food processor, combine the dry ingredients (everything but the butter and milk) and pulse a couple of times until well blended. You can do this in a mixing bowl by using a wire whisk, but a food processor makes this recipe much easier and faster.

4. Add cold butter chunks to the food processor and pulse until the mixture resembles corn meal. Do not over-mix or let the butter get warm. If you are not using a food processor, you can mix the flour and butter together with clean hands, by rubbing it between your fingers. Work quickly if you choose this method.

5. Add half of the buttermilk mixture and stir or pulse to combine. Add more milk until a sticky dough is formed, then empty the bowl onto a countertop or cutting board dusted with flour.

PRO TIP

Make a small indention in the center of your biscuits using your thumb before you bake. This will ensure they rise uniformly.

6. Sprinkle flour on the top and fold the dough over itself left to right, then top to bottom. Flatten the dough slightly and repeat, left over right, top over bottom. Again, resist the urge to over-mix.

7. Flatten the dough to about 1" thick and cut with a biscuit cutter. Place on a baking sheet with the edges touching slightly.

8. Bake for 12-14 minutes. If you like (and you should), take them out halfway through baking and brush the tops with melted butter.

OVERNIGHT OATS

      1/2 cup rolled oats
      1 cup milk
      1 teaspoon chia seeds
      1 tablespoon maple syrup or agave
      2 tablespoons chopped nuts or seeds (optional)
      2 tablespoons dried fruit (optional)

Add all ingredients to a bowl with a tight-fitting lid (you could also use a pint jar) and shake well to mix. Place in the refrigerator overnight. Enjoy right out of the refrigerator or topped with fresh fruit.

INSTANT OATMEAL PACKETS

It's simple to make your own instant oatmeal packs at home in a few minutes.

To begin, put about a cup of dry oats into your food processor or blender and pulse a few times until powdery, then set this aside. Add 1/4 cup of your unprocessed oats into each container, followed by two tablespoons of oat powder. Finish with a pinch of salt in each baggie and you are done! Seriously!

Of course you can add all sorts of flavor variations if you are so inclined. My personal favorite is dried cranberries and pecans, but you might also add dried apples, raisins or whatever else gets you there.

To keep things quick I will usually just stick with the basic recipe and add the flavors and fruit I am in the mood for that morning and *voila!*, homemade instant oatmeal packs that only have the ingredients I put there. They cost less, are better for me and still save just as much time as the pre-packaged version.

Other possible additions include:
      brown sugar
      maple syrup
      nuts
      cinnamon
      chocolate chips
      dried fruit
      anything else you like!

SOUPS

VEGETABLE
BARLEY SOUP

PAGE 28

ROSEMARY WHITE BEAN STEW

2 cans white beans, drained and rinsed
1 small onion, minced
3 cloves garlic, minced
2 teaspoons chopped fresh rosemary
1/2 teaspoon dried oregano
1 1/4 cup vegetable broth (p107) or bouillon (p115)
a cup of fresh spinach
olive oil

1. In a saucepan, sauté onion and garlic in olive oil over medium heat for 3-5 minutes, until soft.

2. Add rosemary and oregano, and cook for an addition minute, stirring to release the oils in the herbs.

3. Add beans and vegetable broth and bring to a boil. Reduce heat and simmer for 15 minutes on low heat. Stir in spinach and simmer for 5 minutes more, until spinach wilts.

4. Taste for seasoning and add salt and pepper as needed.

THAI COCONUT SOUP

1 bunch green onions
1 sweet red pepper, thinly sliced
4 garlic cloves, minced
1" piece of fresh ginger, grated
1 carrot, scrubbed and shredded
1 fresh jalapeño, seeded and minced
2 shiitake mushrooms, sliced
4 cups vegetable broth (p107)
1 tablespoon soy sauce
1 can full-fat coconut milk
the zest and juice of 1 lime
a handful of fresh cilantro
a handful of fresh basil
cooking oil

1. Thinly slice the green onions, separating the white portions from the green.

2. In a saucepan over medium heat, sauté the white part of the onions with the garlic and ginger for 2-3 minutes.

3. Add the rest of the vegetables and cook, stirring often, for another 5 minutes to soften the vegetables.

4. Add the broth, coconut milk, lime juice, and soy sauce and bring to a boil, then reduce the heat to low.

5. Add the herbs and lime zest and taste for seasoning. Add salt and pepper as needed.

TOMATO BASIL SOUP

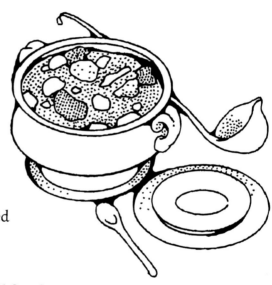

    2 carrots, scrubbed and diced
    1 sweet onion, chopped
    2 cups vegetable broth (p107)
    2 cups milk
    1 cup cashews
    2 large (28oz) cans crushed tomatoes
    a big handful of fresh basil, roughly chopped
    olive oil

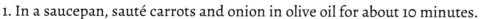

1. In a saucepan, sauté carrots and onion in olive oil for about 10 minutes.

2. Add vegetable broth and basil and bring to a boil.

3. Add canned tomatoes and return to a boil, then reduce heat and simmer for 30 minutes.

4. Combine milk and cashews in a blender and blend until smooth.

5. Remove soup from heat and puree using a stick blender until smooth.

6. Add cashew cream and stir through. Taste for seasoning and add salt and pepper as needed.

SLOW COOKER LENTIL SOUP

1 quart vegetable broth (p107)
2 quarts water
2 cups dried red split lentils
2 cups carrots, cut into 1/4" coins
1-2 cups celery, sliced
1 medium onion, chopped
2-3 cloves garlic, minced
2 bay leaves
1 tablespoon onion powder
1 teaspoon chili powder
1 tablespoon herbs de Provence
2 teaspoons sea salt
pinch of red chili flakes (optional)

1. Place all ingredients in a large slow cooker and stir to combine.

2. Cover, set slow cooker to LOW and allow to cook for 7-8 hours.

3. Taste for seasoning and add salt and pepper as needed.

GAZPACHO

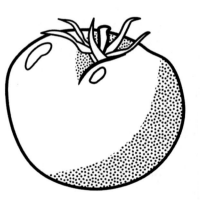

4-5 ripe tomatoes, in season
1 sweet red pepper
1 garlic clove
1 medium cucumber, peeled
1 jalapeño pepper, seeded (optional)
1 tablespoon apple cider vinegar
juice of a lemon
2 tablespoons olive oil

1. Coarsely chop tomatoes, red pepper, and cucumber. Pulse a few times in the blender.

2. Add remaining ingredients up to olive oil and process to a fairly smooth consistency.

3. Taste for seasoning and add salt and pepper as needed.

CREAMY BUTTERNUT SQUASH & TURNIP SOUP

1 butternut squash, peeled and cubed
3 medium turnips, cubed
1 medium sweet onion, chopped
2 bay leaves
 2 sprigs fresh thyme
a handful of fresh parsley, chopped
cooking oil

1. In a stockpot, cover squash and turnips with water. Add bay leaves and thyme.

2. Bring to a boil and reduce heat to simmer. Cook for 15-20 minutes, until vegetables are completely tender.

3. Slowly sauté onion in oil over medium-low heat until they begin to brown just slightly.

4. The goal is to cook off a lot of the moisture from the onions.

5. Remove bay leaves and thyme from cooked vegetables and strain the liquid. Reserve.

6. If you have an immersion 'stick' blender, combine the vegetables and onion in the stock pot with about 1 cup of the cooking liquid. Season with salt & pepper and puree until smooth and creamy.

NOTE: If you use a regular blender, blend 2-3 cups at a time with just a little liquid, and be sure to vent the lid to allow steam to escape.

7. When the vegetables are smooth, stir in the chopped parsley and taste for seasoning. Add salt & pepper as needed.

PASTA FAGIOLI

6 cups vegetable broth (p107)
1 bay leaf
2 cups fresh spinach, packed
2 carrots, diced
4 Roma tomatoes, chopped
1 small onion, chopped
3 garlic cloves, minced
8 oz shell pasta
2 cans navy beans
olive oil

1. Add broth, bay leaf, spinach, carrots and tomatoes to crock pot. Cover and set to high heat.

2. Sauté with onion and garlic in olive oil. Add to crock pot, cover and leave it alone for 2-3 hours, or until carrots are tender but not mushy.

3. In a saucepan, boil pasta and drain.

4. Add pasta and beans to crock pot and set to low heat for 30 minutes.

5. Taste for seasoning and add salt and pepper as needed.

VEGETABLE BARLEY SOUP

2 cups vegetable broth (p107)
1/4 cup uncooked pearled barley
1 carrot, chopped
1/2 medium onion, chopped
2 cloves garlic, minced
1 stalk organic celery, chopped
1 cup kale, chopped
1 small turnip, diced into 1/4" cubes
2 tablespoons tomato paste
1/4 cup cherry tomatoes, halved (optional)
olive oil

1. Cook barley according to package instructions and set aside.

2. In a soup pot, heat 2 tablespoons olive oil over medium heat and sauté onions, carrots, turnip and celery for 5 minutes until onions become translucent and carrots have softened slightly.

3. Add garlic and cook for an additional 60 seconds, stirring constantly.

4. Stir in tomato paste until fully incorporated, then stir in vegetable broth and 2 cups of water.

4. Add remaining ingredients, including cooked barley. Bring to a low boil, then reduce heat and simmer for 30 minutes.

5. Taste for seasoning and add salt and pepper as needed.

CARROT GINGER SOUP

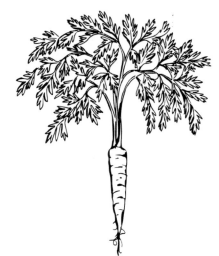

    1 tablespoon vegan butter
    1 medium onion, chopped
    1 1/2 lbs. carrots, peeled and diced
    1" fresh ginger, grated
    2 teaspoons coriander seeds, crushed
    4 cups vegetable broth (p107)

1. Sauté the onions in butter until translucent.

2. Add carrots, ginger and coriander and stir over medium heat for 5 minutes.

3. Add broth and reduce heat, simmering for 30 minutes.

4. Purée using a stick blender. Taste for seasoning and add salt and pepper as needed.

CREAMY BROCCOLI SOUP

cooking oil
1 sweet onion, chopped
1 russet potato, peeled and chopped
3 cups milk, divided
3 cups vegetable broth (p107)
3 cups chopped broccoli

1. In a saucepan over medium heat, sauté onion in oil until soft.

2. Add remaining ingredients (except salt and pepper) and bring to a boil. Reduce heat and simmer for 15 minutes.

3. When potatoes are fork tender, remove from the heat and puree with a stick blender, or carefully, in small batches in a regular blender.

4. Return to saucepan over low heat. Taste for seasoning and add salt and pepper as needed.

SLOW COOKER CHILI

1 large can diced tomatoes
1 can garbanzo beans
2 zucchini, diced coarsely
2 stalks celery, chopped
1 bell pepper, chopped
1 onion, chopped
2 carrots, diced
2 tablespoons chili powder
1 teaspoon garlic powder
1 teaspoon onion powder
1 jalapeño, diced finely
2 cloves garlic, minced
2 cups water

1. Combine all ingredients in a crock pot, stir, cover and cook on low for 6-8 hours.

2. Taste for seasoning and add salt and pepper as needed.

KITCHEN SINK SOUP

All ingredients are optional. Use what you've got on hand.

1 carrot, diced
1 zucchini, diced
1 tomato, peeled and diced
1 large onion (or 2 medium), diced
1 cup whole corn
1 cup cabbage , chopped
1 can chickpeas or white beans
1 clove garlic, minced
1 tablespoon oregano
1 tablespoon rosemary
water
vegetable broth (p107)
wine

1. Sauté onion and garlic in a stock pot over medium heat.

2. Add carrots and cabbage and sauté for another 5 minutes.

3. Add 4 cups of water or broth and remaining ingredients, bring to a boil.

4. Add 4-5 cup of liquid (any combination of water, vegetable stock, and/or wine) and simmer for at least one hour before serving.

5. Taste for seasoning and add salt and pepper as needed.

SPLIT PEA SOUP

1 lb uncooked split peas
1 large onion or 2 leeks
2 stalks celery
2 cloves garlic, chopped
4 cups water
2 cups white wine
pinch cayenne pepper

1. In a stock pot, sauté onion, celery and garlic.

2. Add water and wine, peas and cayenne and bring to a boil.

3. Reduce heat and simmer 25 minutes or until peas are done.

4. Transfer half of the soup to a blender and purée until smooth.

5. Return to pot and heat on low.

6. Taste for seasoning and add salt and pepper as needed.

CREAMY POTATO LEEK

1 1/2 lbs potatoes, peeled and diced
2 cups water or vegetable broth
2 tablespoons nondairy margarine
2 leeks, white portion only, thinly sliced
2 cups milk
cashew cream cheese (optional)
chives (optional)

1. Sauté leeks or onions in margarine.

2. Add remaining ingredients, bring to a boil and reduce heat, simmering until potatoes are tender.

3. Allow to cool and ladle half of the mixture into the blender and purée.

4. Return to saucepan and mix. Warm gently and serve with cream cheese and chives on top.

5. For an interesting addition, top this hearty soup with:

leftover hash browns
roasted peppers
diced jalapeños
salsa

ROASTED PEPPER SOUP

    5 red bell peppers
    1 tablespoon olive oil
    1 onion, chopped
    2 cloves garlic, minced
    6 cups vegetable broth (p107)
    1 teaspoon thyme
    dash Tabasco sauce

1. To roast peppers, cut them in half, remove seeds and inside membrane and place them cut side down on a baking sheet sprayed with cooking spray. Broil until the skin is charred and dark, then remove the peppers from the oven and put them in a sealed container to steam for 10-15 minutes. Peel and coarsely chop peppers.

2. Sauté onions, garlic in oil.

3. Pureé onions, garlic and peppers with broth and return to stock pot.

4. Bring to a boil then reduce heat to low and simmer for 10 minutes, stirring occasionally.

5. Taste for seasoning and add salt and pepper as needed.

SLOW COOKER BLACK BEAN SOUP

    2 cans black beans
    1 cup whole kernel corn
    1 cup chopped onion
    1 clove garlic, minced
    1/2 lemon, juiced
    1 small can tomato paste
    1 teaspoon oregano
    1 teaspoon parsley
    1 teaspoon rosemary
    1 teaspoon black pepper
    1 teaspoon sea salt
    2 1/2 cups water or vegetable broth

Add all ingredients to crock pot, cover and cook on low heat for 6-8 hours.

BLACK BEAN CORN CHOWDER

2 cans black beans, drained and rinsed
1 can diced tomatoes
1 can whole kernel corn, drained
1/2 cup water
2 tablespoons chili powder
1 teaspoon cumin powder
1 clove garlic, minced

1. Toss everything in the crock pot and cook on low for 8 hours or high for 4 hours. I know you want it to be more complicated than that, but just do it, ok?

2. Taste for seasoning and add salt and pepper as needed.

ROASTED CORN CHOWDER

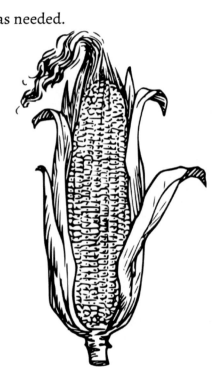

4 ears of sweet yellow corn
cooking oil
2 Russet potatoes, peeled and diced
1 carrot, peeled and finely diced
2 celery ribs, finely diced
1 medium sweet onion, diced
2 garlic cloves, minced
4 cups vegetable broth (p107)
1 cup milk (soy or almond work best)
1/4 cup fresh parsley, finely chopped

Preheat oven to 425F.

1. Shuck the corn and brush with oil. Sprinkle with salt and place on a baking sheet lined with parchment paper. Roast for 30 minutes, turning halfway through.

2. In a large stockpot, heat ¼ cup oil over medium heat. Add onion, carrot & celery and sauté for 2 minutes.

3. Add garlic and potatoes, stir to coat with oil and cook for 5 minutes, stirring constantly. Add vegetable broth, stir, and reduce heat to a simmer. Partially cover and simmer for 10 minutes, or until the potatoes are fork tender.

4. Using a sharp knife, cut the corn kernels from the cob. They will be slightly dry, making the process a lot easier and less messy. Reserve the kernels from 1 ear of corn, placing the rest in the stock pot. Add milk and parsley and stir to combine.

6. CAREFULLY ladle the mixture into a blender, filling the blender only about 1/3 full. **It is very important that the hot mixture is allowed to vent steam or you're going to have a big mess on your hands (and all over your kitchen). If your blender lid has a removable center, take it out and cover the lid with a folded kitchen towel.** Pulse the mixture a few times to break everything down then blend until smooth and velvety.

7. Repeat the process until all of the soup is blended. Taste for seasoning and add salt and pepper as needed. Ladle soup into bowls, garnish with a sprinkle of parsley & the reserved corn kernels, and serve.

MOROCCAN KALE GARBANZO STEW

    1 tablespoon olive oil
    1 medium onion, chopped
    2 garlic cloves, minced
    1 cinnamon stick
    2 teaspoons ground coriander
    3 teaspoon ground cumin
    1/2 teaspoon cayenne
    1 can diced fire-roasted tomatoes in their juice
    4 cups vegetable broth (p107)
    1 medium sweet potato, peeled and cubed
    1 1/2 teaspoons kosher salt
    1 can garbanzo beans with liquid
    2 cups chopped kale, stems removed

1. Heat the oil in a large, heavy bottomed pot over medium heat. Add the onion and garlic and sauté for about 5 minutes or until tender. Stir in the cinnamon, coriander, cumin, and cayenne and cook for 2-3 minutes until the spices are fragrant.

2. Add the diced tomatoes and their juice, chicken broth, butternut squash and potato and bring to a boil. Season with kosher salt. Reduce the heat to a simmer and cook for about 30 minutes or until the squash and potatoes are fork tender.

3. Stir in the garbanzo beans and chopped kale and simmer for 5 minutes or until chickpeas are warmed through and the kale starts to wilt. Garnish with cilantro leaves and serve.

SALADS

QUINOA
TABBOULI

PAGE 38

QUINOA TABBOULI

1 cup quinoa
4 Roma tomatoes, finely chopped
1 large cucumber, peeled and chopped
2 bunches parsley, finely chopped
4 green onions, finely chopped
juice of 2 lemons
4 tablespoons extra virgin olive oil
salt

1. Cook the quinoa according to package instructions.

2. While the quinoa cooks, combine tomatoes, cucumbers, parsley, and green onions in a mixing bowl. Add the cooled quinoa and stir to combine.

3. Add lemon juice and olive oil and stir well. Refrigerate for a few hours before serving.

PICNIC CHICKPEA SALAD

1 can chickpeas, drained (save the aquafaba)
1/2 medium sweet onion, finely chopped
1 medium apple, finely cubed
3 tablespoons pecans, chopped
Aquafaba Mayo (p108)
a pinch of cayenne pepper

1. Rinse the chickpeas and transfer them to a mixing bowl.

2. Using a fork or large spoon, mash the chickpeas just until there are no whole peas left.

3. Stir in remaining ingredients until well mixed.

4. Taste for seasoning and add salt and pepper as needed.

MINT MELON SALAD

    2 cups honeydew melon, chunked
    2 cups cantaloupe, chunked
    1/3 cup fresh mint, chopped
    2 tablespoons lime juice
    2 tablespoons agave nectar

1. Combine all ingredients and stir well to mix.

2. Refrigerate for at least 2 hours prior to serving to allow flavors to meld.

SUMMER PASTA SALAD

    2 cups rotini or macaroni
    1 cup whole kernel corn
    2 cups chopped broccoli florets
    1 medium cucumber, diced
    1 1/2 cups finely diced sweet pepper
    1 pint cherry tomatoes, halved
    1 cup chopped red onion
    1 medium carrot, shredded
    1 cup sliced black olives
    1 1/2 cups Italian dressing (p98)
    large handful fresh parsley

1. Cook rotini according to package directions for al dente. (That means if the package says to cook it for 8-10 minutes, you should take it off after 8 minutes.)

2. Drain and run under cool water to stop the pasta from cooking any further.

3. In a large bowl, add pasta and the remaining ingredients and toss well to mix. Taste for seasoning and add salt and pepper as needed.

4. Refrigerate at least two hours (preferably overnight) before serving.

CUCUMBER SALAD

2 cucumbers, peeled and sliced, then cut into quarter slices
1 pint grape tomatoes, halved
1 medium red onion, chopped
1 teaspoon dried dill
1/4 cup apple cider vinegar
1/4 cup olive oil

1. Combine all ingredients in a mixing bowl and toss to combine.

2. Taste for seasoning and add salt and pepper as needed.

3. Refrigerate overnight before serving.

FOOD RESCUE POWER SALAD

This is my go-to make ahead salad. I can make a big batch on the weekend for an easy grab-and-go lunch all week.

1 bunch kale, de-ribbed and finely chopped
1 cup cooked quinoa
1 cup chickpeas
1 cup tomatoes, chopped
1 bunch spring onions, chopped
1 carrot, shredded
1/4 cup dried cranberries
1/4 cup sunflower seeds

1. Add all ingredients to a large mixing bowl and mix until well combined.

2. Toss with your favorite dressing.

CORN SALAD

     1 bag frozen corn
     3 tablespoons apple cider vinegar
     1/4 cup olive oil
     1 red bell pepper, chopped
     1/2 red onion, chopped
     1 bunch green onions, chopped
     1/2 bunch of fresh parsley, chopped

1. Add all ingredients to a large mixing bowl and mix until well combined.

2. Add vinegar and oil and mix well.

3. Taste for seasoning and add salt and pepper as needed.

4. Refrigerate for at least an hour before serving.

AMAZING CAESAR SALAD

     1 head Romaine lettuce, chopped
     Roasted Chickpeas (p111)
     Caesar Dressing (p98)
     nutritional yeast
     black pepper

This one's pretty self-explanatory. You have lettuce, crunchy chickpea croutons, and Caesar dressing. Top it with nutritional yeast and black pepper and you're good to go.

SIDES

MAC, NO
CHEESE

PAGE 47

CILANTRO LIME RICE

4 cups of pre-cooked rice (brown rice is healthiest)
juice of 1 lime
a handful of fresh cilantro, chopped

1. Add juice and finely chopped cilantro to the rice and stir it well to combine.

2. Cover and allow flavors to meld for 15 minutes before serving.

PRO TIP
You can make your own vegan bacon bits using the recipe for Eggplant Bacon in the Breakfast chapter!

GERMAN POTATO SALAD

2 pounds new potatoes (I prefer Yukon gold)
1 small onion, diced
vegan bacon bits
1/2 cup vegetable stock
1/4 cup apple cider vinegar
1 Tablespoon dried dill weed
1 small bunch chives, minced

1. Cut potatoes in half and boil in salted water for 15-20 minutes, just until fork tender. Drain and return to pan.

2. Sauté onion in oil until soft.

3. Add stock, vinegar, and potatoes and toss together. Simmer until liquid is absorbed.

4. Stir in bacon, dill, and chives. Taste for seasoning and add salt and pepper as needed.

5. Serve warm.

SOUTHERN PICNIC POTATO SALAD

2 pounds red-skinned potatoes
1/4 cup Aquafaba Mayo (p108)
1/4 cup of sweet onion, finely minced
1 celery rib, finely minced
3 tablespoons sweet pickle relish
1 teaspoon dry mustard
2 teaspoons paprika, plus extra

1. Cut potatoes in half and boil in salted water for 15-20 minutes, just until fork tender. Drain and transfer to mixing bowl to cool for 15 minutes.

2. Add remaining ingredients and toss well to combine.

3. Taste for seasoning and add salt and pepper as needed.

4. Sprinkle paprika on top of the finished dish.

SOUTHERN PICNIC SLAW

1 pound white cabbage, sliced very thin
1 medium carrot, grated
1 small sweet onion, grated
3 tablespoons light cooking oil
1/4 cup sugar
1/2 cup apple cider vinegar
2 Tablespoons Dijon mustard
1 teaspoon celery seed

1. Place cabbage, carrot, and onion in a large mixing bowl and stir to mix evenly.

2. In a small saucepan, combine remaining ingredients and cook over medium heat until sugar is dissolved. Pour over vegetables and stir to combine well.

3. Cover and refrigerate for at least an hour, preferably overnight.

SLOW COOKER 'REFRIED' BEANS

    16 oz. dried pintos (about 2 cups)
    6-8 cups water
    1 onion, chopped
    1 tablespoon Taco Seasoning mix (p119)
    1/2 pickled jalapeño, coarsely chopped (optional)
    2 teaspoons granulated garlic
    1 teaspoon black pepper
    2 teaspoons salt

1. The night before, rinse and sort dried beans and add to the slow cooker. Cover with 6 cups of water and allow to soak until morning.

2. Drain beans and return them to the slow cooker. Add water and remaining ingredients, and stir.

3. Cover and set your slow cooker on low heat. Cook for 5-7 hours on low, or until beans are fork tender.

4. Drain beans over a large bowl or pot to keep the cooking liquid.

5. Using a wooden spoon or potato masher, mash the beans until they are the desired consistency. Add reserve liquid as needed and freeze the leftover liquid (called pot liquor) for adding to soups or stews later.

SESAME GREEN BEANS

    1 pound fresh green beans
    cooking oil
    1 tablespoon sesame seeds
    1/2 cup vegetable broth (p107)
    1 teaspoon sesame oil

1. Heat a nonstick pan over medium heat. Toast sesame seeds, stirring constantly, until golden.

2. Add 2 tablespoons of oil and stir in green beans. Cook until the beans brighten in color, then add broth and cover. Cook for 8-10 minutes, until beans become tender.

3. Remove lid and allow remaining liquid to evaporate. Stir in sesame oil.

4. Taste for seasoning and add salt and pepper as needed.

MAC, NO CHEESE

This recipe is for my no cheese sauce, and it assumes you already know how to boil pasta. I mean, c'mon...pasta? I don't recommend making the finished dish ahead of time, but you can make and refrigerate the sauce for up to a week, and just stir it into hot pasta when you're ready to eat.

    2 cups Russet potato, peeled and cubed
    1 cup carrot, scrubbed and diced
    1 cup onion, coarsely chopped
    1 cup cashews
    4 cloves garlic
    1 cup nutritional yeast
    1 cup milk (I use soy)
    2 tablespoons apple cider vinegar
    2 tablespoons tapioca starch/flour (optional, adds to the stretchy behavior)
    1 teaspoon onion powder
    1/2 teaspoon smoked paprika
    1 1/2 teaspoon salt
    1/3 cup oil

PRO TIP

Add a few pickled jalapeno slices to the no cheese sauce for the best nacho dip you've ever tasted.

1. Boil potato, carrot, onion, and cashews for 8-10 minutes, or until carrot is fork-tender. Drain.

2. Add ingredients to a high powered blender and blend on high speed until smooth and creamy.

NOTE: If you don't have a high powered blender, it may be easiest to process the sauce in two batches.

3. To make the perfect Mac, No Cheese, add 1 cup of sauce for every 8 ounces of cooked pasta.

4. This is best when served immediately.

ROASTED BRUSSELS SPROUTS

    1 pound fresh Brussels sprouts
    olive oil
    salt

Preheat oven to 425F.

1. Wash Brussels sprouts and trim away excess stem. Cut in half and transfer to a small mixing bowl.

2. Drizzle halves with olive oil until very lightly coated. Sprinkle with salt and spread evenly on a baking sheet lined with parchment or silicon mat.

3. Bake for 30-35 minutes, turning midway through, until roasted and tender.

EDAMAME

    1 1/2 cups edamame
    olive oil
    1/2 teaspoon chili powder
    1/4 teaspoon onion powder
    1/4 teaspoon garlic powder
    1/4 teaspoon cumin
    pinch paprika
    1/8 teaspoon dried basil

Preheat oven to 375F.

1. Place edamame in a mixing bowl and drizzle with olive oil, tossing to coat evenly.

2. Add seasonings and spices and mix well to cover all of the edamame.

3. Spread on a cookie sheet in a single layer and bake for 10-12 minutes, stirring every 3-4 minutes, until beans are just beginning to brown.

4. Allow to cool for a minute or two before serving.

CREAMY GARLIC MASHED POTATOES

  2 pounds Yukon gold potatoes, cut into 3/4-inch cubes
  3 cloves garlic, minced
  4 tablespoons vegan butter
  1/4 cup nutritional yeast
  2 tablespoons fresh chives or parsley
  1 cup milk

1. Place cut potatoes in a saucepan and cover with cold water. Bring to a boil, then reduce heat and simmer for 12-15 minutes, or until fork tender. Drain and return to the pan.

2. Add remaining ingredients and mash with a potato masher until your desired consistency is reached. Add more milk as needed.

3. Stir in chives, taste for seasoning and add salt and pepper as needed.

SAUTÉED CAULIFLOWER

  1/2 head of cauliflower
  olive oil
  1 clove garlic, minced
  chives
  lemon zest

1. Clean and chop cauliflower into bite sized pieces.

2. Heat olive oil in a pan and add garlic, tossing to coat.

3. Cook until the edges begin to brown then add garlic, cooking for another 2 minutes.

4. Remove from heat and stir in remaining ingredients. Taste for seasoning and add salt and pepper as needed.

MUSHROOM PATE WITH PECANS AND RED WINE

2 big handfuls of dried oyster or porcini mushrooms
2 large fresh portobello mushrooms
1 cup pecans
1 cup water
2 cups red wine
2-3 sun-dried tomatoes
1 tablespoon soy sauce
2 sprigs fresh rosemary
2 tablespoons olive oil

1. Boil water and pour it over dried mushrooms in a heat-safe bowl or small sauce-pan. Allow to steep for about 30 minutes.

2. At the same time, cover pecans with water and allow to soak.

3. Strain soaked mushrooms through cheesecloth to remove grit, reserving soaking liquid.

4. Coarsely chop portobellos and add to a pan along with soaked mushrooms, tomatoes, rosemary, red wine, and soy sauce. Simmer over medium heat until liquid has evaporated, then add soaking liquid and simmer until that liquid is also evaporated.

5. Remove from heat, discard rosemary sprigs, and allow mushrooms to cool for at least 30 minutes.

6. Drain pecans and pulse in a food processor until pulverized.

7. Add the cooked mushrooms, black pepper, and olive oil, and process until smooth and light. Taste for seasoning and add salt & pepper to taste.

8. Refrigerate until well chilled, for up to 2 days before serving.

BAKED POTATO WEDGES

6 Russet potatoes cut into 6-8 equal wedges, lengthwise
4 tablespoons oil
4 tablespoons flour
2 teaspoons onion powder
3 teaspoons of garlic powder
2 teaspoons paprika
1 teaspoon salt
1 teaspoon black pepper

Preheat oven to 450F.

1. Place cut potatoes in a mixing bowl and add oil. Toss to coat the wedges completely.

2. Combine remaining ingredients in a zipper bag. Add a few wedges at a time and toss to completely coat.

3. Line coated potatoes on a baking sheet and bake for 40-45 minutes, turning the potatoes halfway through the baking.

4. Sprinkle hot potatoes with a little salt and allow to cool for a few minutes before serving.

ENTREES

MARINARA
PAGE 100

CRISPY EGGPLANT
MEDALLIONS

PAGE 73

SPRING & SUMMER ROLLS

All ingredients are optional. Use what you like:

> spring roll wrappers
> cabbage
> leftover rice noodles
> vegetables of your choice (I love carrots, beets & parsnips)
> sprouts
> fresh basil or cilantro
> avocado
> Thai Peanut Sauce (p101)

1. Start with a plate, bowl, or baking dish that is larger than the wrappers. Add a little water to the container and set aside.

2. Shred cabbage, julienne or finely slice the vegetables, and thinly slice the avocado.

3. One at a time, place a wrapper in the container of water, flipping it after a few seconds to wet the entire wrapper. When the wrapped begins to become flexible, remove it from the container and transfer it to a cutting board, wiping away the excess moisture.

4. Add ingredients one at a time across the center of the wrapper, in lines from left to right, leaving about an inch and a half of empty space at both ends.

5. Wrap the left and right sides toward the center. Pull the wrapper end closest to you up and over the filling, and roll it tightly toward the other end.

6. Cut rolls in half and serve with Thai Peanut Sauce or other dipping sauce of your choosing.

BURRITOS

When it comes to on-the-go meals, they don't get much easier than this. Bring together any combination of the following that make you happy:

> flour tortillas
> refried beans (p46)
> black beans
> shredded lettuce
> diced tomato

roasted corn
shredded vegan cheese
diced onion
salsa (p109)
tofu
guacamole (p109)
cashew sour cream (p99)
rice

1. Down the center of a flour tortilla placed on a plate or cutting board, spread half of the beans, lettuce, tomatoes, cheese, diced onions and other ingredients of your liking.

2. Fold the end closest to your body away from you about 2 inches, then fold the left side inward about two thirds of the way, then the right side inwards to form a pocket. Roll away from you to finish the burrito. (it may take a few tries to get the hang of it, but don't give up!)

3. Top with salsa and serve.

FIESTA BOWLS

cooked brown rice
black beans or pinto beans (I like both)
chopped tomatoes
lettuce
whole kernel corn
diced cucumbers
jalapeños
cilantro
salsa (p109)
cashew sour cream (p99)
guacamole (p109)
fresh lime juice

Start your bowl with rice and beans, then pile on the other ingredients that you like, leaving off the stuff that doesn't make you happy. *Easy!*

BLACK BEAN & SWEET POTATO QUESADILLAS

This is a great way to use leftovers, and it's so easy I'm not even going to make it look like a recipe. All you have to do is mash some sweet potato and black beans onto a flour tortilla, sprinkle on a little cumin, salt & pepper, and cover with a second tortilla. Then cook over **low heat** in a nonstick skillet for a couple of minutes on each side. Keep the temperature low and you won't burn your quesadilla.

Finish by cutting into quarters and serve with salsa.

If you've got leftover corn, onion, beefless crumbles, or whatever else strikes your fancy, toss 'em on. Got some vegan shreds? Get busy!

CREAMY CAULIFLOWER ROASTED VEGETABLES

> 3-4 cups cooked brown rice
> 1/2 head of cauliflower, cut into manageable pieces
> 1 cup non-dairy milk
> 2 medium zucchini, sliced into ½" coins
> 2 carrots, cut into 1" pieces
> 1 medium turnip, cut into 1" cubes
> 1 purple onion, quartered with the root still intact (to keep it together)
> 3 cloves garlic
> olive oil
> salt and pepper
> 1/4 cup nutritional yeast

Preheat the oven to 425F.

1. Place zucchini, carrots, turnip, and onion in a large mixing bowl and toss to coat with olive oil. Spread on a baking sheet and sprinkle with salt & pepper.

2. Tear a small sheet of aluminum foil and place the garlic cloves in the center. Drizzle olive oil. Sprinkle with salt & pepper and fold the aluminum foil into a small packet. Add to the baking sheet.

3. Roast for 30 minutes. Remove the garlic packet and check vegetables for doneness. Continue to cook in 5 minute intervals as needed.

6. While the vegetables are roasting, boil the cauliflower in a medium saucepan for 10 minutes, or until tender. Drain.

7. Transfer cauliflower, roasted garlic, non-dairy milk, and 1/2 teaspoon of salt to a blender. Blend on high speed until creamy.

8. When vegetables are done, stir creamy cauliflower sauce into the brown rice and divide into 2 bowls. Top the rice with the roasted vegetables and serve!

BASIC VEGETABLE CURRY

Like the name says, this is basic. Use this as a springboard, and include your favorite ingredients.

> 1 yellow onion, diced
> 4 cloves garlic, minced
> olive oil
> 2 carrots, scrubbed and diced
> 1 russet potato, peeled and diced
> 1" piece of fresh ginger, grated
> 1 can chickpeas, drained and rinsed
> 2 tablespoons Curry Powder (p117)
> ½ teaspoon salt
> 1 can diced tomatoes
> 1 can coconut milk

1. Sauté onions and garlic in oil until translucent.

2. Add carrots, potatoes, and ginger and cook for another 3 minutes.

3. Stir in remaining ingredients and bring to a boil. Reduce heat and simmer for 15 minutes.

4. Serve on its own or on a bed of rice.

DAL & COCONUT RICE

1 cup brown rice, uncooked
1 cup lentils
1 medium onion, chopped
2 carrots, scrubbed and diced
2 cloves garlic, minced
2 teaspoons cumin, divided
1 teaspoon coriander
1 teaspoon chili powder
 1 bay leaf or a pinch of ground bay
1 can diced tomatoes
2 cups rice, cooked
1 cup coconut milk
olive oil

1. In a saucepan, sauté onion and garlic in olive oil until translucent. Add carrots and cook for another 2 minutes.

2. Combine 2 cups water with lentils and other ingredients (1 teaspoon cumin) through bay leaf and bring to a boil. Reduce heat and simmer for about 20-25 minutes stirring occasionally, until lentils are done, adding water as needed.

3. In a separate saucepan while the lentils cook, add cooked rice, 1 teaspoon cumin and coconut milk. Heat through and keep warm until ready to serve.

4. Add diced tomatoes and season to taste with salt & pepper.

5. Serve lentils atop rice with cooking liquid poured over the top.

HUMMUS & FUL

I owe my love for this dish to a restaurant in Decatur, Georgia called Lawrence's. It's literally just a plate of hummus and ful medames, which are a simple but tasty fava bean recipe. The flavor is amazing, and when you bring these two recipes together, something magical happens.

hummus
1 can fava beans
olive oil
2 cloves garlic, minced
1 teaspoon ground cumin
juice of 1 lemon
fresh flat-leaf parsley, chopped

1. In a saucepan, sauté the garlic in olive oil for a minute or so, then add the cumin and stir.

2. Add fava beans, lemon juice, and salt & pepper to taste. Simmer on low heat for 10-15 minutes to allow the flavors to come together.

3. Serve atop a generous portion of hummus and sprinkle liberally with fresh chopped parsley.

FALAFEL

PRO TIP

Refrigerating the chopped mixture will make it easier for them to form into balls.

    1/2 pound dried chickpeas
    1 cup fresh chopped cilantro & parsley
    1 small bunch of green onions
    2 cloves garlic, minced
    2 teaspoons salt
    1 teaspoon ground cumin
    cooking oil

1. Rinse and sort chickpeas and soak overnight in cool water. Drain and toss chickpeas in a towel to dry the surface.

2. Combine all ingredients through cumin in a food processor and pulse just until ingredients are uniformly chopped.

3. Gently form into balls no larger than a golf ball in size and flatten them slightly.

4. Fry in hot oil roughly two minutes per side until browned. Transfer to a draining rack or a plate lined with paper towels to drain.

EASY LASAGNA ROLLS

lasagna noodles
marinara
Pure Abundance Artisan Vegan Cheese (see p122) or cashew cheese
beefless crumbles
fresh parsley
nutritional yeast
garlic powder

Preheat oven to 350F.

1. Cook the noodles according to package instructions.

2. Spread a thin layer of your chosen ingredients on each noodle, then carefully roll them before placing them in a 9x13 pan on top of a layer of marinara.

3. Bake for 25 minutes.

ALGIO E OLIO

1/4 cup olive oil, plus extra
8 garlic cloves, minced
1 tablespoon crushed red pepper flakes (optional)
1/4 cup nutritional yeast
1/4 cup fresh parsley, chopped
roasted cherry tomatoes (p111)
spaghetti

1. Cook pasta according to package directions. Reserve half cup of cooking liquid.

2. In a pan, heat a quarter cup of the oil. Sauté garlic over medium heat until slightly browned. Add pepper flakes and reserved liquid and allowed to cook for 2 minutes.

3. Toss pasta in pan until combined, adding more oil if needed.

4. Sprinkle parsley and nutritional yeast on pasta and toss to combine. Add salt and pepper to taste.

5. Top with roasted cherry tomatoes and serve.

CALZONES

 1 recipe pizza dough (p112)
 marinara (p100)
 vegan cheese
 pizza fillings

Preheat oven to 475F.

1. Divide a standard pizza dough recipe into four equal parts and form into balls. On a floured surface, flatten dough balls into1/4" discs about a foot across.

2. Add a few tablespoons of sauce on the right half of the dough leaving an inch of dry space around the outer edge.

3. Add your choice of fillings, careful not to stuff them too full or they'll burst while baking.

4. Dampen the outer edge of the circle, fold the left half over the right and press the edges together firmly to create a pocket. Transfer to a baking sheet lined with parchment paper.

5. Brush with olive oil and bake for 15-18 minutes, until the tops become lightly golden.

6. Remove from the oven and allow to cool for 10 minutes before serving with a small bowl of warm marinara sauce for dipping

STEAMED ZUCCHINI NOODLES
WITH RAW TOMATO SAUCE

2 medium zucchini
2 medium tomatoes, cored and quartered
1 sweet red pepper, stem and seeds removed, coarsely chopped
2 cloves garlic, finely minced
½ medium sweet onion, coarsely chopped
½ small Serrano pepper (optional), stem and seeds removed
handful of fresh basil, thinly sliced
juice of half a lemon or lime

1. Use a mandolin slicer or Spiralizer to cut the zucchini into thin noodles. You can use a knife if that's all you've got, but it will take a while.

2. In a blender or food processor, combine the onion, garlic, sweet pepper, and Serrano pepper. Pulse until well-chopped and combined.

3. Add tomatoes, basil, and lime and pulse until the mixture is well-blended but still slightly chunky.

4. Pour into a fine mesh strainer positioned over a bowl and allow to drain for 15-30 minutes. Reserve the liquid to add to a future juice.

5. To serve, place zucchini noodles in a bowl and top with plenty of sauce. Garnish with extra basil leaves.

6. Steam the noodles using a vegetable steamer if you have one, or boil them for 45 seconds, immediately removing them from the water

RED BEANS & RICE

1 can dark red kidney beans
1 cup brown rice, uncooked
1 medium sweet onion, chopped
1 medium sweet pepper, chopped
1 fresh jalapeño, thinly sliced
1 cup cherry tomatoes, halved
4 tablespoons tomato paste
2 tablespoons Taco Seasoning (p119)
oil

1. To cook brown rice perfectly, bring 8 cups of salted water to a rapid boil and stir in the rice. reduce heat to medium and allow to boil for 30 minutes. Drain, return to saucepan and cover. Allow to sit undisturbed for 10 minutes.

2. Sauté onion and peppers in oil over medium heat until they soften slightly. Add tomato paste and taco seasoning and stir to combine.

3. Add tomatoes and cook for 2-3 minutes, stirring constantly. Add water as needed to create a thick sauce.

4. Drain and rinse red beans and add them to the vegetable mixture. Stir and simmer for 10 minutes. Taste for seasoning and add salt and pepper as needed.

5. To serve, add rice to a bowl and top with red beans, vegetables, and sauce.

NOODLE BOWLS

2 tablespoons miso paste
2 cloves of garlic, minced
1 tablespoon Seasoned Salt (p114)
1 tablespoon soy sauce
1 tablespoon sesame oil (optional but delicious)
4 cups vegetable broth (p107)
rice vermicelli noodles or similar
1 carrot, julienned

1/4 sweet red pepper, sliced into thin strips
2 tablespoons fresh basil, thinly sliced
1/2 block of firm tofu, cubed
2 tablespoons chopped peanuts or cashews (optional)

1. Cook noodles according to package instructions.

2. In a saucepan, add ingredients through broth and heat to boiling.

3. Add carrot, red pepper, basil, and tofu and reduce heat. Simmer for 5 minutes.

4. For each serving, add noodles to a large bowl, top with vegetables and ladle in broth as desired.

5. Garnish with chopped nuts and serve with chili oil or sriracha.

FRIED RICE

2 cups brown rice, cooked
cooking oil
1/2 medium yellow onion, chopped
4 cloves garlic, minced
1" fresh ginger, grated
2 medium carrots, scrubbed and diced
1 cup mushrooms, quartered
1 cup frozen peas
1 teaspoon onion powder
1 teaspoon garlic powder
1 tablespoon soy sauce
kala namak black salt (optional, for light egg flavor)
3 green onions, thinly sliced

1. In wok or large frying pan, sauté onion, garlic, carrots, and mushrooms for 5 minutes.

2. Transfer to a large mixing bowl, add rice, peas, onion powder, garlic powder, and soy sauce. Mix thoroughly.

3. Add 3 tablespoons of oil to the pan and set to medium heat.

4. Add mixture to hot pan and press flat with a large spoon or spatula. Cook for 2 minutes, undisturbed.

5. Life an edge of the mixture to ensure that the rice is beginning to turn golden in color, then stir the rice and continue to cook for another 5 minutes, stirring occasionally.

6. Serve garnished with green onion and add more soy sauce as needed.

TACO MAC

2 cups macaroni noodles
2 cups meatless crumbles
2 tablespoons Taco Seasoning (p119)
1/8 cup water
No Cheese sauce (p47)
olive oil

1. Cook macaroni according to package instructions and drain.

2. Sauté crumbles over medium high heat in a little oil for 2-3 minutes.

3. Add taco seasoning and water, stir, and continue to cook over medium heat until the liquid reduces.

4. Add cooked macaroni and nacho cheese and stir. Cover and allow to sit for 5 minutes before serving.

KETCHUP

PAGE 108

DREAM BURGERS

PAGE 69

THE AMAZING NUT BURGER

1/2 cup finely chopped walnuts
1/2 cup sunflower seeds
1 cup canned chickpeas, drained
1/4 cup diced red onion
3 tablespoons aquafaba
fresh parsley
2 tablespoons olive oil

1. Toast walnuts and sunflower seeds in a dry skillet over medium heat for about 5 minutes.

2. Mash garbanzo beans and add onion, egg, parsley, and toasted nuts.

3. Add salt, pepper and seasoning and mix.

4. Form mixture into patties.

5. Fry in olive oil 2-3 minutes each side, or until brown and done.

PRO TIPS
Instead of a traditional bun, why not serve these in an open pita?

Uncooked burgers will keep refrigerated for 3-4 days, or up to 2 weeks in the freezer. Simply thaw and fry for a quick meal anytime.

BLACK BEAN BURGERS

1 can black beans
1 sweet onion, chopped
2 tablespoons quick cooking oats
1/4 cup chopped parsley
3 tablespoons aquafaba
splash of milk
flour

1. Mash beans and add remaining ingredients (except flour).

2. Shape into patties by forming balls and flattening them. Thinner patties will cook best.

3. Refrigerate until ready to cook, then dredge lightly in flour and sauté in oil over medium heat until golden.

THE DREAM BURGER

A few, simple ingredients along with a simple process results in one of the best plant-based burgers I have ever eaten, much less made at home. The texture is unbelievable, and they freeze like a dream, so go ahead and make lots!

 1 tablespoon flax seeds
 4 tablespoons warm water
 1 can pinto beans
 1 medium zucchini, coarsely chopped
 2 garlic cloves
 6-8 small button mushrooms
 1/2 cup sunflower seeds
 2 teaspoons Seasoned Salt (p114)
 1/2 cup nutritional yeast
 1/2 teaspoon cayenne (optional, but recommended)
 1 cup all-purpose flour
 1/2 cup red bell pepper

Preheat oven to 375F.

1. Add flax and water to a small bowl and stir. Allow to sit for 5 minutes.

2. Add all ingredients to a food processor and process until all chunks are gone.

3. Lightly oil a baking sheet and scoop 1/3 cup of mixture at a time onto the sheet, using moistened fingers to flatten and shape them into patties.

4. Bake for 15 minutes, then flip the burgers carefully and bake for an additional 5 minutes.

NO MEAT LOAF

 1 cup Textured Vegetable Protein (TVP)
 1 cup gluten
 1 cup rolled oats
 1 small onion, minced
 1 carrot, shredded

3 tablespoons onion flakes
1 teaspoon chili powder
2 teaspoons salt
1/2 teaspoon black pepper
1 tablespoon parsley flakes
1 tablespoon garlic powder
1 tablespoon onion powder
1/2 tablespoon oregano
1 tablespoon Poultry Seasoning (p115)
1 teaspoon dry mustard
1/2 cup nutritional yeast
2 teaspoon liquid smoke
1 1/2 cups boiling water
1 cup crushed tomatoes
ketchup (p108)

Preheat oven to 350F.

1. In a large mixing bowl, combine dry ingredients (everything through nutritional yeast) and stir or whisk together to thoroughly combine.

2. Add onion, carrot, liquid smoke, water, and crushed tomatoes and mix well.

3. Lightly coat a loaf pan with cooking spray or line with parchment paper, and press the mixture into the pan.

4. Cover with a layer of ketchup, sprinkle with salt & pepper and bake for 90 minutes.

5. Remove from the oven and allow to cool for one hour for best results.

To freeze: Cool completely, wrap in aluminum foil and seal in a freezer bag. Keeps for 3 months.

SHEPHERD'S PIE

2-3 cups mashed potatoes (great use for leftovers)
2 cups meatless crumbles
1 medium onion, diced
1 cup whole kernel corn
1 cup carrots, finely diced
1 cup frozen peas
2 tablespoons all-purpose flour
2 tablespoons vegan butter
1 cup broth made with Beefless Bouillon (p115)
1 teaspoon garlic powder
1 teaspoon onion powder
paprika
nutritional yeast

Preheat oven to 400F.

1. Melt butter in a pan and whisk in flour. Continue stirring for 1 minute.

2. Add beefless broth and bring to a boil, stirring constantly. Reduce heat and simmer for 2 minutes.

3. Add crumbles, onion, carrots, peas, and corn to the sauce and mix thoroughly.

4. Spread mixture in a casserole dish and top with mashed potatoes. Sprinkle with vegan shreds (if using), salt, pepper and a bit of paprika.

5. Bake for 30 minutes.

PANCAKES

PAGE 17

CRISPY EGGPLANT MEDALLIONS IN MARINARA

cornstarch
1/4 cup aquafaba
1 cup bread crumbs
1 teaspoon dried parsley
1 teaspoon dried oregano
1/2 teaspoon salt
1/4 teaspoon garlic powder
1 small eggplant cut into 1/4" slices
vegetable oil
1 pint marinara sauce (p100)
Pure Abundance Artisan Vegan Cheese (see p122) or cashew cheese

1. In a saucepan set to medium heat, add marinara sauce and about 1/4 cup of Pure Abundance. Stir to combine and allow to heat through.

2. Meanwhile, arrange three bowls on the counter:
    1)cornstarch
    2)aquafaba
    3)breadcrumbs, parsley, oregano, salt, & garlic powder, combined.

2. Press the eggplant slices between paper towels or clean kitchen towels to remove moisture, then coat each with cornstarch, aquafaba, and bread crumbs.

3. Fry in oil over medium heat for 60-90 seconds per side, until golden, then drain on paper towels.

4. Serve with marinara and crumbled Pure Abundance cheese on top.

A WORD ABOUT SEITAN

Seitan is a versatile, protein-rich meat alternative made from vital wheat gluten. As that implies, people with Celiac disease will unfortunately not be able to enjoy the tasty benefits of seitan. Still, it is an important tool for those without gluten tolerance issues to have in their arsenals, so I am including the following recipes for those who can get down with the gluten.

COUNTRY FRIED SEITAN

> 1 recipe Basic Seitan (p106)
> all-purpose flour
> 1/2 cup aquafaba or 1 tablespoon of flax meal mixed with water
> cooking oil
> Country Gravy (p103)

1. Start with the basic seitan recipe. When the dough is finished, pull or cut it into smaller pieces and flatten out into patties roughly the size of a burger.

2. Proceed with the recipe instructions to cook.

3. Add some flour, salt & pepper to one bowl, and about ½ cup aquafaba to another. With a whisk or a fork, lightly whip the aquafaba until frothy.

4. With the seitan patties fully cooked, coat them in flour, dip into the aquafaba, then back into the flour to coat.

5. Pan fry in oil over medium heat until golden brown.

6. Top generously with country gravy and serve.

PRO TIPS

Serve your Country Fried Seitan on Better Than Buttermilk Biscuits.

BUFFALO SEITAN NUGGETS

1 recipe Basic Seitan (p106)
all-purpose flour
1/2 cup aquafaba or 1 tablespoon of flax meal mixed with water
cooking oil
salt and pepper
1/2 cup coconut oil
2/3 cup hot pepper sauce
1 1/2 tablespoons vinegar
1/4 teaspoon garlic powder
1/2 teaspoon smoked paprika

1. Start with the basic seitan recipe. When the dough is finished, pull or cut it into bite size pieces and proceed with the recipe instructions to cook.

2. Add some flour, salt & pepper to one bowl, and about ½ cup aquafaba to another. With a whisk or a fork, lightly whip the aquafaba until frothy.

3. With the seitan nuggets fully cooked, coat them in flour, dip into the aquafaba, then back into the flour to coat.

4. Pan fry in oil over medium heat until golden brown.

5. Whisk together melted coconut oil pepper sauce, vinegar, garlic powder, and paprika and dip hot nuggets into the sauce before serving.

6. Serve with your favorite sauces or dips (there are plenty to choose from in the Dressings & Sauces chapter).

NOTE: You can use the same method with the patties made in the previous recipe for a crazy good Buffalo Seitan sandwich. Try it on a Better Than Buttermilk Biscuit!

STORE BOUGHT MEAT ALTERNATIVES

Okay, let's address the elephant in the room. Store bought meat alternatives are a thing. They weren't really a big deal when I was a young vegan, because tofu and TVP were pretty much all there was. Now, thanks to companies like Gardein, Beyond Meat, Field Roast, and others, there are some delicious and surprisingly convincing alternatives for everything from ground beef to chicken tenders, and then some.

Even with the knowledge and experience that I have in the kitchen, I always have a couple of bags in the freezer that I can use to throw together a quick meal. That's why I wanted to include a few of my favorite recipes that incorporate meat alternatives that have been purchased at the store.

Please note that I don't use these highly processed foods often, and I don't suggest that you do, either.

FISHLESS TACOS

> Gardein™ Fishless Filets or similar brand
> shredded cabbage
> pickled onions (p112)
> tartar sauce (p107)
> taco shells

1. Prepare Fishless Filets according to package instructions. When cooked, slice diagonally into four pieces each.
2. Line each taco shell with cabbage, onion, filet slices, and tartar sauce.

MONGOLIAN BEEFLESS BROCCOLI

1/2 cup soy sauce
1/2 cup water
3/4 cup dark brown sugar
2 teaspoons vegetable oil
1 tablespoon garlic, minced
2 tablespoon corn starch, dissolved in ¼ cup cool water
2 large green onions, chopped
1 package Gardein™ Sizzling Szechuan Beefless Strips or similar brand
1 pound broccoli crowns

1. Discard sauce packet and cook the Beefless Strips according to package instructions.

2. To make the sauce, heat vegetable oil and sauté garlic in a small pan for 60 seconds over medium heat.

3. Add soy sauce, water, and brown sugar and stir to combine fully. Bring to a boil and reduce heat to medium low. Allow to reduce for 2-3 minutes, then turn off the heat and stir in the corn starch to thicken.

4. Steam broccoli crowns for 8-9 minutes until just tender.

5. When Beefless Strips are cooked, toss them in sauce, and pour the remainder over the broccoli, tossing to coat.

6. Add a handful of chopped green onion just before serving, with rice on the side.

BEEFLESS TIPS WITH ROASTED VEGETABLES IN A RED WINE REDUCTION

1 medium sweet onion, chopped
1 pint of button mushrooms, chopped
4 cloves of garlic, minced
2 celery ribs, finely chopped
4 carrots, scrubbed and cut into thick coins
5 cups Beefless Bouillon (p115)
2 medium potatoes (I like Russet for this), scrubbed and cubed
2 teaspoons dried oregano
1/2 teaspoon ground dry mustard
2 bay leaves or 1/4 teaspoon ground bay leaves
1 package Gardein™ Beefless Tips or similar brand

1. Sauté onion, mushrooms, garlic, celery, & carrot in oil over medium heat for about 5-7 minutes, or until the onions are translucent.

2. Transfer cooked vegetables to the slow cooker and add remaining ingredients. Stir to combine.

3. Slow cook on low heat setting for 4-6 hours.

4. Taste for seasoning and add salt and pepper as needed.

GENERAL TSO CHICK'N

1 3/4 cups water
1/2 cup soy sauce
1/2 cup white vinegar
1/4 cup red wine
3/4 cup sugar
1/8 cup cornstarch
3 cloves garlic, minced
pinch of cayenne pepper
1 tablespoon poultry seasoning (p115)
1 Thai chili or 1 tablespoon crushed red pepper flakes
2 tablespoons oil
1 medium sweet onion, sliced thin
1 medium sweet red pepper, sliced
1 package Gardein™ Seven-Grain Crispy Tenders or similar

1. Prepare tenders according to package directions.

2. Make the sauce by placing for 10 ingredients (through red pepper flakes) in a blender and blending until well-combined.

3. In a large skillet, heat olive oil over medium heat and sauté onion and pepper until onions are translucent and peppers are fork tender.

4. Add sauce and cook, stirring constantly, until sauce thickens to desired consistency.

5. Toss tenders in to coat and serve over steamed rice.

DESSERTS

**PERFECT
CHOCOLATE CAKE**

PAGE 89

ZUCCHINI CHOCOLATE CHIP MUFFINS

    1 1/2 tablespoons ground flax
    4 tablespoons water
    1 cup sugar
    1/2 cup vegetable oil
    1 cup raw zucchini, grated
    1 teaspoon vanilla
    1 1/2 cups all-purpose flour
    1/2 teaspoon baking soda
    1/2 teaspoon salt
    1/4 teaspoon baking powder
    1/2 cup chopped pecans or walnuts
    1/2 cup dark chocolate chips

Preheat oven to 350F.

1. In a small bowl, mix flax and water and set aside.

2. In a mixing bowl, whisk together flour, soda, salt, and baking powder.

3. Add sugar, oil, zucchini and vanilla and stir to mix.

4. Stir in nuts and chocolate chips and pour into muffin tins lined with paper cups or coated with cooking spray.

5. Bake for 20-25 minutes, until they pass the toothpick test.

SIMPLE RICE PUDDING

    1 cup brown rice, uncooked
    1 1/4 cups unsweetened milk (coconut milk works great)
    1/2 teaspoon vanilla
    1/2 teaspoon cinnamon
    1/3 cup sugar or maple syrup
    raisins (optional)

1. Cook brown rice according to package instructions.

2. Stir in remaining ingredients and cook over low heat until the liquid is absorbed. Top with raisins (if desired) and serve.

CRANBERRY NUT BREAD

2 cups all-purpose flour
1 cup sugar
1 teaspoon salt
1/2 teaspoon baking soda
1 1/2 teaspoons baking powder
1/2 cup vegan butter
1 teaspoon freshly grated orange zest
3/4 cup fresh orange juice
3 tablespoons aquafaba
1 cup cranberries, chopped
1/3 cup walnuts, chopped

Preheat oven to 350°F.

1. In a large mixing bowl, whisk together flour, sugar, salt, baking soda, and baking powder until combined. Add butter using your fingers or a pastry blender and combine to form a texture like meal.

2. In a separate mixing bowl, add the aquafaba and whisk briskly for about 2 minutes, or until foamy, then add to the bowl of dry ingredients.

3. Stir in orange zest and juice until just combined (don't over mix).

4. Fold in cranberries and walnuts and pour mixture into a loaf pan prepared with parchment, vegan butter, or cooking spray.

5. Bake for 75-90 minutes, until a toothpick inserted in the center comes out clean.

MUD SHAKES (KID APPROVED!)

1 cup almonds
1 tablespoon raw cacao powder
2 bananas
6 soft, pitted dates
2 cups milk

Just put all the ingredients in the blender and blend until smooth!

PUMPKIN CHAI BREAD

6 tablespoons aquafaba
1 1/2 cups all-purpose flour
2 teaspoons baking powder
1/2 teaspoon baking soda
1/2 teaspoon salt
1 teaspoons cinnamon
1/2 teaspoon nutmeg
1 cup canned pumpkin (not pumpkin pie mix)
1/4 cup vegetable oil
1/2 cup sugar
1/2 cup cold chai (p11)
1 teaspoon vanilla
1/2 cup walnuts, chopped (optional)
1/2 cup dark chocolate chips (optional)

Preheat oven to 350F

1. In a large mixing bowl, whisk together flour, baking powder, baking soda, cinnamon, nutmeg, and salt.

2. Whisk aquafaba in a separate bowl until frothy, then stir in pumpkin, oil, sugar, chai, and vanilla until smooth.

3. Add the wet ingredients to the dry and fold until just combined. If you're adding nuts or chocolate, fold those in now.

4. Pour into a prepared loaf pan and bake for 45 minutes, or until a toothpick inserted in the center comes out clean.

POUND CAKE WITH GLAZE

1 1/2 cups all-purpose flour
1 1/2 teaspoons baking powder
1 teaspoon baking soda
1/2 teaspoon salt

1/4 cup milk
1/4 cup vegetable oil
2/3 cup sugar
1/2 block silken tofu, drained
1/2 tablespoon vanilla

Preheat oven to 350F and prepare a loaf pan with cooking spray and a light dusting of flour.

1. Whisk dry ingredients (the first four) in a mixing bowl until well combined.

2. Add remaining ingredients to a blender and blend until creamy.

3. Add the wet ingredients into the dry a little at a time and fold them in until combined.

4. Pour the mixture into the prepared pan and bake for 25-30 minutes, until a toothpick inserted in the center comes out clean.

6. Allow to cool for 15 minutes before removing from the pan.

For the glaze:

Whisk together 1/2 cup powdered sugar, 1/2 teaspoon vanilla, and a tablespoon of milk until smooth. Drizzle over pound cake when the cake has completely cooled.

DATE NUT ENERGY BITES

2 cups nuts & seeds
2 cups dates, pitted
1 tablespoon cacao powder
a good pinch of salt
1 1/4 cups unsweetened shredded coconut, divided

1. Process nuts and seeds in a food processor until well chopped and crumbly.

2. Add remaining ingredients (save ¼ cup coconut) and pulse until the mix forms a sticky ball.

3. Scoop the dough out and roll into balls that are a little smaller than a golf ball.

4. Roll balls in the remaining coconut and place in a sealed container.

5. Refrigerate for at least 2 hours before serving.

FRUIT COBBLER

When it comes to making cobbler, you have plenty of room to get creative. Use the fruit – or combination of fruits – you like. You'll need roughly 6 cups of actual fruit, so if you're using canned, drain the liquids into a bowl before you measure.

Save the liquid, though, as you may use it.

>   6 cups of fruit
>   1 cup all-purpose flour
>   1 cup sugar
>   8 tablespoons vegan butter, at room temperature
>   pinch of salt
>   1 tablespoon corn starch (optional)

Preheat oven to 350F.

To make the topping:

1. In a mixing bowl, combine flour, sugar, and butter and stir until well combined. The mixture should come together easily into a ball, otherwise add a bit more flour.

2. Pour fruit into a 9"x13" baking dish. If you want the fruit filling to be less juicy, add a tablespoon of cornstarch to a cup of reserved fruit liquid and pour it over the fruit.

3. Crumble the cobbler topping over the dish in a fairly even manner, but don't worry about being too exact.

4. Place baking dish on a baking sheet to catch any drips or bubble-overs and bake for 45-55 minutes, until the topping is golden brown and the fruit filling is bubbling.

PEANUT BUTTER COOKIES

1 tablespoon ground flax
3 tablespoons water
1/2 cup vegan butter
1/2 cup natural granulated sugar
1/3 cup packed dark brown sugar
1 teaspoon vanilla
3/4 cup peanut butter
1 2/3 cup all-purpose flour
1 teaspoon baking soda
1/2 teaspoon salt

Preheat oven to 350F.

1. In a small bowl, combine flax and water and stir. Set aside while you ready the remaining ingredients.

2. Using a mixer, beat the butter and sugars for 2-3 minutes, until light and airy. Add the vanilla and peanut butter and mix until combined.

3. In a separate bowl, whisk together the dry ingredients (flour, soda, salt). Slowly add dry ingredients to the wet and stir until just mixed. Be careful not to overmix. Place the bowl in the freezer for 15 minutes.

4. Form the cookies by scooping out roughly a tablespoon of dough and rolling them into a ball.

5. Place on a baking sheet and flatted using a fork to form the familiar pattern. Be sure to leave the cookies room to expand when they bake.

6. Bake for 10-12 minutes, until the edges are slightly brown and the cookies are a golden color.

7. Cool for 5 minutes on the sheet before transferring to a cooling rack.

CHOCOLATE CHIP COOKIES

1 cup vegan butter
3/4 cup brown sugar, packed
1/4 cup white sugar
1 teaspoon vanilla extract
1 1/2 cups all-purpose flour
1/2 teaspoon salt
1 teaspoon baking soda
1/4 cup unsweetened milk
2 cups quick-cooking oats
1 1/2 cups dark chocolate chips

Preheat oven to 350F.

1. Using a mixer, beat butter, sugar and vanilla until fluffy.

2. In a separate bowl, whisk together flour, salt, and baking soda.

3. Mix wet and dry ingredients and stir in milk, oats, and chocolate chips.

4. Drop by the spoonful onto a baking sheet and bake for 10-12 minutes.

5. Cool for 5 minutes on the sheet before transferring to a cooling rack.

CHOCOLATE PUDDING

3 tablespoons cornstarch or arrowroot powder
3 tablespoons water
1 3/4 cups unsweetened milk
1/4 cup cocoa powder
1/4 teaspoon salt
1/4 cup sugar or maple syrup
1/2 teaspoon vanilla extract

1. Combine cornstarch and water in a small cup and stir to form a slurry, then combine all ingredients with the slurry in a saucepan over medium high heat and bring to a low boil, stirring constantly.

2. Lower heat to medium and continue to cook (and stir) for 3-4 minutes, as the mixture thickens. Remove from heat and transfer to fridge-safe containers. Chill for 2 hours before serving.

THE PERFECT CHOCOLATE CAKE

2 1/2 cups flour
2 cups sugar
2/3 cup cocoa powder
2 teaspoons baking soda
1 teaspoon salt
1 cup water
1 cup milk (I use soy)
2 teaspoons vanilla extract
2/3 cup vegetable oil
2 teaspoons apple cider vinegar (you can use white in a pinch)

Preheat oven to 350F.

1. In a mixing bowl, combine flour, sugar, cocoa, baking soda, and salt. Whisk to combine and remove all lumps.

2. Whisk in water, milk, vanilla, oil, and vinegar until well combined.

3. Prepare the cake pan with cooking spray and cocoa powder, and pour in the batter.

4. Bake for 40-45 minutes, or until a toothpick comes out clean.

5. Cool for 15 minutes, then invert over a cake plate and remove from pan (skip if you're making cupcakes, or using a sheet cake pan.)

CHOCOLATE GLAZE

Don't start the glaze until the cake is completely cooled and ready to be iced!

1/2 cup sugar
4 tablespoons vegan butter
2 tablespoons milk
2 tablespoons unsweetened cocoa powder
2 teaspoons vanilla extract

1. Add all ingredients to a saucepan and heat over medium high heat, whisking constantly to keep mixture from scorching.

2. Once the mixture melts and begins to bubble, lower the heat slightly to medium and continue to whisk as it reduces. In 5-10 minutes, the glaze will thicken slightly and will take on a creamy consistency. That's when you'll know it is ready to use.

3. QUICKLY pour the glaze over cake and allow to cool for about 5 minutes.

NOTE: For easier cleanup, add hot water to your saucepan as soon as you're finished, otherwise the glaze will become one with the pan, and you will never separate them again.

BANANA NUT BREAD

1 tablespoon ground flax
3 tablespoons water
1 1/2 cups all-purpose flour
1 teaspoon baking soda
1/2 teaspoon salt
1 cup sugar
3 medium ripe bananas
1 cup chopped pecans or walnuts (optional)
1/3 cup vegetable oil
1 teaspoon vanilla extract

Preheat oven to 375F.

1. In a small bowl, combine flax and water and set aside.

2. In a mixing bowl, whisk together dry ingredients (flour, soda, salt) to combine.

3. In a separate bowl, mash bananas with sugar, oil, vanilla, nuts (if using), and flax mixture.

4. Fold the wet ingredients into the dry until just mixed.

5. Pour into prepared muffin tins to 3/4 full and bake for 20-22 minutes until they pass the toothpick test.

DRESSINGS & SAUCES

DRESSINGS

I have never understood why people buy salad dressing. Don't get me wrong, I love them too, I just don't know why anyone would spend a lot of money buying a bottle of something that they can easily make at home in a couple of minutes, for a few pennies.

The salad dressings in this chapter are so easy, most of them don't even have instructions. All you really need to make a top shelf dressing is a whisk, a bowl, a list of ingredients, and a few minutes. Not to worry, though - any recipes that need more than a whisk or a shake will be explained in detail. As a rule, I mix then taste for seasoning and add salt and pepper as needed at the end, which is why they aren't always listed as ingredients.

VINAIGRETTES

Vinaigrettes are so simple, delicious, and infinitely versatile that you could make one every day and never have the same thing twice. There's a reason why nearly every restaurant makes their own. Not only are they fresher and more flavorful, they're really inexpensive. It all comes down to remembering an easy ratio, and from that foundation you can create your own masterpieces.

Create a base by starting with 1 part acid and 3 parts fat/oil, then let your imagination go wild. You may find (as I do), that you want more zing in your dressing. Add more acid. Or, if you want a particular dressing to have a sweeter flavor, add a drizzle of maple syrup to the mix.

Keep it simple by using vinegar and olive oil, or go crazy and replace your acid with grapefruit juice, and your oil with avocado. The important thing to remember is to whisk the acid and fat together well. And don't forget to add something fresh when you have it. Minced garlic or ginger, fresh herbs, whatever makes you smile. Here are a few of my favorite combos to get you started:

CLASSIC BALSAMIC VINAIGRETTE

> 2 tablespoons balsamic vinegar
> 6 tablespoons olive oil
> 1 tablespoon minced fresh herbs

SPICY CITRUS VINAIGRETTE

2 tablespoons grapefruit juice
6 tablespoons vegetable oil
1/2 tablespoon maple syrup
pinch of cayenne pepper

ASIAN-INSPIRED VINAIGRETTE

2 tablespoons rice wine vinegar
5 1/2 tablespoons vegetable oil
1/2 tablespoon sesame oil
1 teaspoon fresh minced ginger
soy sauce

LEMON VINAIGRETTE

1/4 cup red wine vinegar (apple cider will work in a pinch)
2 tablespoons Dijon mustard
1 teaspoon dried oregano
1 clove garlic, minced
1/2 cup canola oil

AVOCADO LIME

1 ripe avocado
1 clove garlic, minced
1/8 cup milk
juice of half a lime
fresh cilantro or parsley, minced
drizzle of olive oil (optional)

Add all ingredients to a blender and process until smooth and creamy. Taste for
seasoning and add salt and pepper as needed.

RANCH

2 tablespoons Ranch Mix (p117)
1 tablespoon vinegar
1 cup Cashew Sour Cream (p99)

1/4 cup milk

CATALINA

1/4 cup ketchup
1/4 cup maple syrup
1/4 cup apple cider vinegar
1 teaspoon onion powder
splash of vegan Worcestershire sauce

THOUSAND ISLAND

1/2 cup Aquafaba Mayo (p108)
2 tablespoons ketchup
1 tablespoon white vinegar
2 teaspoons sweet relish
1 teaspoon sweet onion, minced
1/4 teaspoon garlic powder
2 teaspoons sugar

SESAME GINGER

1/4 cup water
1/2 cup rice wine vinegar
1/2" piece of ginger, minced
2 tablespoons soy sauce
2 tablespoons maple syrup
2 tablespoons canola oil
2 teaspoons sesame oil
1 teaspoon sesame seeds

GREEN DRAGON

    1 cup Aquafaba Mayo (p108)
    1 ripe avocado
    1/2 cup parsley, finely chopped
    1 teaspoon crushed seaweed (dulse, nori, wakame)
    3 green onions (just the greens)
    1/2 of a jalapeño, seeded and finely minced
    juice of half a lemon

Add all ingredients to a blender and process until smooth and creamy.

LEMON POPPY

    1/4 cup fresh lemon juice
    3/4 cup oil
    1 tablespoon maple syrup
    1 tablespoon Dijon mustard
    1 tablespoon poppy seeds

TOMATO MISO

    1/2 cup diced tomatoes (canned is fine)
    1/4 cup water
    4 tablespoons canola oil
    1/4 cup minced red onion
    2 cloves garlic, minced
    3 tablespoons white vinegar
    3 tablespoons miso paste

Add all ingredients to a blender and process until smooth and creamy.

ITALIAN

2 tablespoons of Italian Dressing mix (p119)
2 tablespoons water
1/3 cup white vinegar
2/3 cup light oil

CAESAR

1 cup Aquafaba Mayo (p108)
2 tablespoons nutritional yeast
2 garlic cloves, minced
2 tablespoons olive brine
1 teaspoon crushed seaweed (dulse flakes, nori, wakame)
2 teaspoons lemon juice

GREEK

1 cup olive oil
1 large lemon, juiced and zested
1 tablespoon garlic powder
1 teaspoon onion powder
1 tablespoon dried basil
1 tablespoon dried oregano
1 tablespoon dried thyme
1 teaspoon ground black pepper

TAHINI DRESSING

1/2 cup tahini
1/2 cup water
juice of half a lemon
1/4 teaspoon garlic powder

SAUCES

A good sauce can make or break a dish. Not only are they really important for flavor and texture, they are great at covering a multitude of sins when mistakes happen in the kitchen - and believe me, they will. I have collected my favorite and most-used sauces here. These are the recipes that I use regularly in my own kitchen, and without them I would be completely lost.

CASHEW SOUR CREAM

    1 cup cashews
    water
    1/2 cup milk
    1 tablespoon vinegar (apple cider is best)
    1 tablespoon lemon juice (fresh, please)
    salt

1. Soak the cashews in water overnight. Drain and transfer cashews to a blender.

2. Add remaining ingredients (except salt) and blend at high speed until thoroughly creamy, scraping down the sides of the blender as needed.

3. Transfer to an air-tight container and taste for salt.

4. The sour cream will thicken as it cools in the fridge (keeps for about a week).

TAHINI SAUCE

    4 tablespoons tahini paste
    juice of a lemon
    1 tablespoon maple syrup
    salt
    warm water

Combine in a small bowl and whisk until smooth, adding warm water a tablespoon at a time until desired consistency has been reached. Taste for seasoning and add salt as needed.

MARINARA

1 large (28 oz) can crushed tomatoes
1 medium sweet onion, minced
2 cloves of garlic, minced
1 teaspoon salt
1 teaspoon maple syrup
1 teaspoon dried parsley
1 teaspoon dried oregano
1 tablespoon vegetable oil
black pepper

1. In a saucepan, sauté onions and garlic in oil over medium heat until soft and translucent.

2. Add remaining ingredients and stir well to combine, while bringing to a boil.

3. Reduce heat and simmer for 30 minutes, or until the flavors come together and the sauce thickens slightly.

4. Taste the sauce and adjust the seasonings to your individual taste.

ALFREDO

1/2 of a medium head of cauliflower, cut into pieces
1 cup cashews
1 cup milk
1/2 of a small onion, chopped
2 cloves of garlic, minced
juice of half a lemon
1/4 cup nutritional yeast
cayenne pepper (optional)

1. Steam cauliflower and cashews for 10 minutes, until cauliflower is soft.

2. Sauté onion in oil until soft. Add garlic and sauté for one minute.

3. Add milk to blender, followed by the rest of the ingredients and blend until smooth.
4. Season with salt and pepper to taste, and toss with pasta to serve.

PESTO

2 cups fresh basil, packed
1/2 cup nutritional yeast
1/2 cup olive oil +/-
1/2 cup pecan halves
juice of half a lemon

1. Pulse pecans in the food processor a few times until they are well chopped.

2. Add basil, 1/4 cup of oil, and lemon juice and pulse a few times.

3. Add nutritional yeast and turn food processor on.

4. Drizzle oil through the opening at the top while the machine is running until the desired creamy consistency is reached.

5. Season with salt and pepper to taste.

THAI PEANUT SAUCE

2 tablespoons soy sauce
1/2 cup creamy peanut butter
1 glove garlic, minced
1" piece of fresh ginger, grated
1 tablespoon fresh lime juice
1 tablespoon maple syrup
crushed red pepper flakes (optional)

1. Combine all ingredients in a mixing bowl and whisk together until well combined.

2. Store in an airtight container in the refrigerator.

HARISSA PASTE

2 red bell peppers
4 jalapeños
6 cloves of garlic
1/4 cup sun dried tomatoes
2 dried chiles
1/2 tablespoon red pepper flakes
2 teaspoons coriander seed
1/2 teaspoon cumin
1/2 teaspoon fennel seed
olive oil
salt and pepper

Preheat oven to 350F.

1. Place dried chiles and tomatoes in a bowl and pour boiling water over them. Let them sit while you prepare the rest of the ingredients.

2. Line peppers on a baking sheet and roast, turning every 10-15 minutes for a total of about 45 minutes, or until roasted dark all around. Remove from oven, cover and allow to cool in the steam.

3. Once cool enough to handle, remove the charred peel and de-seed the peppers and set aside.

4. Drain and de-seed the re-hydrated chiles (wear gloves!) and add them along with the tomatoes and roasted peppers to the bowl of a food processor.

5. In a small pan, dry roast the pepper flakes, coriander seed, cumin, and fennel seed over medium heat for 1-2 minutes, or until lightly fragrant.

6. Add toasted spices to food processor and drizzle in a tablespoon of olive oil.

COUNTRY GRAVY

3 tablespoons vegan butter
1/4 cup all-purpose flour
1 1/2 cups milk

1. Melt butter in a skillet over medium-low heat and whisk in the flour.

2. Allow to cook for about a minute, then add milk a little at a time, whisking until thoroughly incorporated.

3. Taste for seasoning and add salt & pepper as needed.

4. Cook, whisking constantly until gravy reaches the desired consistency.

BROWN GRAVY

3 tablespoons vegan butter
1/4 cup all-purpose flour
1 tablespoon Beefless Bouillon (p115)
2 tablespoons nutritional yeast
1 1/2 cups vegetable broth (p107)
soy sauce
black pepper

1. Melt butter in a skillet over medium-low heat and whisk in the flour.

2. Allow to cook for about a minute, then add broth a little at a time, whisking until thoroughly incorporated.

3. Add bouillon and nutritional yeast and taste for seasoning, adding soy sauce & pepper to taste.

4. Cook, whisking constantly until gravy reaches the desired consistency.

PANTRY STAPLES

**RESTAURANT
SALSA**

PAGE 109

VEGETABLE BROTH

PAGE 107

ITALIAN SEASONING MIX

PAGE 119

I guess you could say we saved the best for last. In this chapter, we are going to talk about the basics – all of the stuff we use regularly but take for granted, because we've bought them at the store for so long. From condiments to flavorful broths to spice blends, this is where I packed all of the tidbits of information that didn't really fit into the regular recipe chapters.

Many of the recipes throughout the book will reference recipes and information from this chapter.

BASIC SEITAN

1 cups vital wheat gluten
1/8 cup nutritional yeast
1/8 cup flour
1/4 teaspoon salt
1 teaspoon turmeric
1 teaspoons onion powder
1 teaspoon garlic powder
1 teaspoon dried sage
1/2 - 3/4 cup broth
1/8 cup soy sauce
1 teaspoons olive oil

1. Bring the stock to a boil, then immediately reduce heat to a low simmer. DO NOT let it boil and stay boiling while the seitan is cooking. Boiled seitan does bad things to the texture, so just don't.

2. Mix the dry ingredients and whisk well. Add the wet ingredients and mix, then knead for about 5 minutes.

3 .Cut the mixture into 4 pieces, that will be roughly the size of a chicken breast when cooked. Flatten them into shape and drop into the stock.

4. Partially cover the pot and let it simmer for 35-45 minutes.

KITCHEN SCRAP VEGETABLE BROTH

This recipe isn't really a recipe, it's a revelation.

To make kitchen scrap broth, you start by saving all of your vegetable and herb ends, skins, and stems (including carrot peels, parsley stems, leftover corn, even apple cores) in a container in the freezer. I can tell you from experience that it doesn't take much time to amass quite an impressive pile of goods.

When you have a good amount (at least a gallon zipper bag full), pile everything in a large stock pot. Add water to cover the scraps, and toss in whatever else you have on hand, such as garlic cloves, dried seasonings, peppercorns, etc.

Turn the heat to medium low and let the magic happen. Resist the urge to let this stuff boil, otherwise you'll end up with a cloudy broth that won't taste as good as if you take your time. This one reason I love to use my slow cooker for this. I can turn it on and let it go for 6 hours on low heat and it's done. All that's left is to strain the liquid through cheesecloth or a mesh nut milk bag, and pour it into containers!

NOTE: I prefer to skip adding salt when I make broth. It isn't really necessary until you're using it in a dish anyway, and I find that I end up using less salt overall.

TARTAR SAUCE

1 cup Aquafaba Mayo (p108)
2 tablespoons sweet pickle relish
1 tablespoon onion, finely minced
2 tablespoons lemon juice or vinegar

Just whisk all of the ingredients together, season with salt to taste, and refrigerate.

SLOW COOKER KETCHUP

    1 large can crushed tomatoes
    1 small onion, chopped
    2 garlic cloves, minced
    1/3 cup vinegar
    1/4 cup brown sugar
    a pinch of allspice
    a pinch of powdered cloves
    1/4 teaspoon ground cinnamon
    1/2 teaspoon dry mustard
    1 tablespoon vegan Worcestershire sauce
    2 tablespoons tomato paste
    2 teaspoons salt

1. Add all ingredients to a slow cooker set on low heat and stir to combine.

2. Allow to cook, covered, for 6-8 hours, until it thickens.

3. Purée the mixture with an immersion blender, or carefully in a regular blender (in batches).

4. Transfer to resealable containers and cool before refrigerating.

AQUAFABA MAYO

Aquafaba is a fancy name for the liquid from a can of chickpeas, and it is a magical thing.

    1/4 cup aquafaba
    3/4 cup canola oil
    2 teaspoons vinegar or lemon juice
    1/2 teaspoon sugar
    1/2 teaspoon salt
    1/2 teaspoon onion powder
    2 teaspoons mustard powder (or Dijon mustard)
    cracked black pepper (optional)

1. Add aquafaba and canola oil to a wide mouth jar (if using a stick blender) or to the blender jar (if using a regular blender). Add vinegar, sugar, salt, and mustard powder.

2. Blend for about a minute, or until smooth and emulsified.

RESTAURANT SALSA

1 large (28 oz) can crushed tomatoes
1 small onion, chopped
1 jalapeño pepper, de-stemmed, de-seeded and chopped
3 cloves garlic, peeled and finely chopped
1 1/2 teaspoons ground cumin, or to taste
juice of 1 lime
a handful of cilantro leaves, chopped

1. Put everything in the blender or food processor and pulse until it reaches an even consistency.

2. Taste for seasoning and add salt as needed.

GUACAMOLE

2 ripe avocados, peeled, seeded
1/2 teaspoon ground cumin
1/2 Roma tomato, seeded & diced
1/4 cup sweet white onion, minced
1/2 jalapeño, seeded & minced
1 tablespoon fresh lime juice
sea salt & cayenne pepper to taste

1. Cut the avocados into large chunks and place them in a bowl. Mash them a bit with a fork (not too much, you want it to be somewhat chunky).

2. Gently mix in the rest of the ingredients and add sea salt and cayenne to taste.

TWO-MINUTE BLACK BEAN DIP

1 can black beans, drained and rinsed
1 teaspoon ground cumin
1 teaspoon chili powder
juice of 1 lime
1/4 teaspoon salt
3-4 pickled jalapeño slices
fresh cilantro, chopped (optional)

Put everything in the blender or food processor and pulse until it becomes mostly creamy.

HUMMUS

1 can chickpeas, drained and rinsed
juice of 1 large lemon
1/4 cup tahini
1 garlic clove, minced
1-2 tablespoons olive oil
1/2 teaspoon ground cumin

Put everything in a food processor and process until it becomes a creamy, thick paste. Add water 1-2 tablespoons at a time if needed to get the right consistency.

ROASTED GARLIC

1 bulb of garlic
1 tablespoon olive oil
salt

Preheat oven to 400F.

1. Peel garlic and transfer to a sheet of aluminum foil.

2. Drizzle with oil, sprinkle with salt, and toss to coat.

3. Fold foil into a packet and roast in the oven for 25 minutes.

ROASTED TOMATOES

1 pint cherry tomatoes
olive oil
salt

Preheat oven to 400F.

1. Halve the cherry tomatoes and place in a bowl.

2. Drizzle just enough olive oil into the bowl to lightly coat.

3. Sprinkle lightly with salt and toss to coat evenly.

4. Spread tomatoes cut side up on a baking sheet lined with parchment.

5. Roast for 20-25 minutes.

ROASTED CHICKPEAS

1 can chickpeas, drained
2 tablespoons vegetable oil
salt

Preheat oven to 450F.

1. Pat the chickpeas dry with a kitchen towel.

2. Add chickpeas to a bowl and toss with oil and salt.

3. Spread evenly on a baking sheet and bake for 30-40 minutes, tossing them half-way through the cooking time to ensure even cooking.

PRO TIP

For a crunchy, protein-rich crouton replacement, add some garlic and onion powder immediately after they come out of the oven.

PICKLED ONIONS

    1 large purple onion
    1 cup water
    1 cup white vinegar
    1/2 cup organic sugar (or sweetener of choice)
    2 teaspoons salt

1. Place water, vinegar, sugar, and salt in a saucepan and heat to boiling.

2. While you wait, peel the onion and use a mandoline slicer or a sharp knife to thinly slice it into rings.

3. Cut the slices in half to split the rings, and carefully pack them into a quart sized jar.

4. Pour the pickling brine over the onions in the jar. If you need more liquid, top it off with hot water.

5. Screw on the lid and allow to cool to room temperature.

Once you have completed these five steps, the pickled onions are ready to eat, but I recommend refrigerating and serving them cold. They'll keep for months covered in the fridge. You can use this basic recipe to pickle other vegetables as well, including cucumbers, matchstick carrots, and radishes. Experiment and see what you can come up with!

PIZZA DOUGH

    2 1/4 teaspoons (1 packet) active yeast
    1 cup of warm water
    2 tablespoons olive oil
    3 cups flour +/- (all-purpose works, so will bread flour)
    1 teaspoon garlic powder
    1 teaspoon salt

When making dough, measurements can never be exact. The consistency you are looking for is one where the ingredients when mixed will form a soft ball. It should not be dry when mixed, but not overly wet either. It will be sticky, so a little oil on your hands will make it easier to work with.

To be honest, I use a bread machine on the dough cycle to do this mixing for me. If you don't have a bread machine, a stand mixer or good old fashioned elbow grease will work just fine. When the ingredients are mixed well, transfer the dough to a bowl that has been rubbed with oil or cooking spray and cover. Let the dough rise until doubled in size, usually about 30 minutes.

When the dough has risen, punch it down and divide into two balls. On a floured surface, knead the dough until it becomes elastic and pliable, then stretch the dough to the desired size for your pizza and place it on a pan or pizza stone to be dressed with sauce and your favorite toppings.

PIE AND PASTRY DOUGH

1 1/2 cups all-purpose flour
9 tablespoons of vegan butter
1/2 teaspoon salt
1/2 teaspoon sugar
bowl of ice water

1. Cut butter into small pieces and place in the freezer for 15 – 30 minutes before beginning the recipe.

PRO TIP

It is imperative that the ingredients be as cold as possible when you are working with them, as this is what will help to keep the pie crust light and flaky.

2. Combine flour, salt and sugar in a food processor and pulse a few times to mix the ingredients thoroughly.

3. Add cold butter to the food processor and pulse it for a few seconds at a time, until the mixture becomes crumbly.

4. Add 3 tablespoons of ice water and pulse until it is fully incorporated. Check the consistency of the dough by picking up a small handful and squeezing it in the palm of your hand. If it holds together, move on to the next step. If not, add more water, one tablespoon at a time, until it does. Be careful not to add too much water, as this will make a tough dough.

6. Pour the dough mixture out onto a lightly floured surface and press it together with the heels of your hands a few times. Then press the mixture together until it forms a rounded disk.

7. Wrap the dough in plastic wrap and place it in the freezer for 15 minutes if you are planning to continue on with making the pie immediately. You can leave it wrapped and frozen for up to 3 days before using it.

SPICE BLENDS

When it comes to indispensable parts of the kitchen, herbs and spices are at the top of the list. You would hardly believe the number of options you can create by changing only the seasonings you use, transforming a few basic ingredients into a variety of dishes.

The seasoning blends in this chapter are the result of a lot of trial and error, but they represent what I feel is some of the most important work I have done in the kitchen. Making your own seasoning and spice blends is not only less expensive than buying at the store, it's insanely empowering to a new cook. Once you've mastered a few basic combinations, you'll never freak out over being out of curry powder or taco seasoning again.

If you don't already have one, I recommend investing in a good spice grinder, basically an inexpensive coffee grinder that is devoted specifically (and only) to grinding herbs and spices. To make the blends in this chapter, simply combine the ingredients listed in an air-tight container and give it a good shake to combine.

HOUSE SEASONING

4 tablespoons salt
1 tablespoon garlic powder
1 tablespoon black pepper

SEASONED SALT

4 tablespoons salt
1/2 tablespoon onion powder
1/2 tablespoon garlic powder
2 tablespoons paprika
1 tablespoon black pepper

LEMON PEPPER

1 tablespoon
zest of 3 lemons, dehydrated
3 tablespoons black pepper

BEEFLESS BOUILLON

1 tablespoon salt
1 tablespoon paprika
1 tablespoon onion flakes
1/2 tablespoon garlic powder
1/4 teaspoon allspice
2 teaspoons dry mustard
3 tablespoons dehydrated mushrooms
1 tablespoon Montreal Seasoning
3 bay leaves
2 teaspoons cacao
1/2 tablespoon black pepper

PRO TIP
Turn bouillon into broth by combining 1 tablespoon of mix per cup of boiling water.

VEGETABLE BOUILLON

2 tablespoons salt
1 teaspoon black pepper
1 teaspoon turmeric
3 tablespoons dried parsley
2 tablespoons garlic powder
1 1/2 tablespoons onion powder
2 teaspoons sage
2 teaspoons thyme
2 teaspoons lemon pepper

POULTRY SEASONING

1 1/2 tablespoons salt
1/2 tablespoon onion powder
1/2 tablespoon garlic powder
1 tablespoon sage
1/4 tablespoon paprika
1/2 tablespoon oregano
1/2 tablespoon thyme
1/4 tablespoon black pepper

MONTREAL SEASONING

2 tablespoons salt
2 tablespoons black pepper
1 tablespoon granulated garlic
1 tablespoon onion flakes
2 tablespoons paprika
1 tablespoon red pepper flakes
1 tablespoon dill

SWEET BARBECUE SEASONING

1 teaspoon paprika
1/2 teaspoon garlic salt
1/4 teaspoon sugar
1/4 teaspoon onion powder
1/4 teaspoon chili powder
1/8 teaspoon ground mustard
dash cayenne pepper

BARBECUE SPICE RUB

1/2 cup brown sugar
1/2 cup paprika
1 tablespoon ground black pepper
1 tablespoon salt
1 tablespoon chili powder
1 tablespoon garlic powder
1 tablespoon onion powder

SAUSAGE SEASONING

2 tablespoons salt
1 tablespoon black pepper
1 tablespoon garlic powder
1 tablespoon onion powder
[continues on next page]

1/8 teaspoon fennel seed
1 tablespoon sage
1 tablespoon thyme
1 tablespoon basil
1/2 tablespoon marjoram
1 teaspoon cayenne (optional, for spicy sausage)
1/4 teaspoon crushed red pepper flakes (optional, for spicy sausage)

RANCH MIX

1/2 cup dried parsley
1 teaspoon garlic powder
4 tablespoons onion flakes
1 teaspoon paprika
1 teaspoon onion powder
1 tablespoon dill
1 teaspoon black pepper
1/2 teaspoon cayenne pepper

CURRY POWDER

1 tablespoon salt
1 tablespoon garlic powder
1 tablespoon onion powder
3 tablespoons chili powder
2 tablespoons cumin
2 tablespoons coriander
1/2 tablespoon turmeric
1 tablespoons smoked paprika
1 tablespoon dry mustard
1 tablespoon cayenne

ONION SOUP MIX

1/4 cup onion flakes
1 teaspoon onion powder
2 tablespoons Beefless Bouillon (p115)
1 teaspoon parley
1/2 teaspoon celery seed
1/2 teaspoon sugar
1/2 teaspoon paprika
1/2 teaspoon black pepper

DORITOS-INSPIRED SEASONING (Original Style)

1/2 teaspoon salt
1/4 cup nutritional yeast
1 1/2 teaspoons chili powder
1 teaspoon garlic powder
1 teaspoon smoked paprika
1/2 teaspoon onion powder

DORITOS-INSPIRED SEASONING (Ranch Style)

1/2 teaspoon salt
1/4 cup nutritional yeast
1 teaspoon chili powder
1 teaspoon garlic powder
1/2 teaspoon smoked paprika
1/2 teaspoon onion powder
1 teaspoon dill
1 teaspoon parsley flakes
1/2 teaspoon dried lemon zest

ITALIAN DRESSING MIX

1 tablespoon garlic powder
1 tablespoon onion powder
1/2 tablespoon dehydrated onion
1 tablespoon white sugar
2 tablespoons dried oregano
1 teaspoon ground black pepper
1/4 teaspoon dried thyme
1/2 tablespoon dried basil
1/2 tablespoon lemon zest
1 tablespoon dried parsley
1/2 teaspoon celery seed
1 teaspoon dill weed
1 tablespoon salt

TACO & FAJITA SEASONING

1 teaspoons salt
7 teaspoons cumin
5 tablespoons chili powder
1 1/4 teaspoons garlic powder
1 1/4 teaspoons onion powder
1 1/4 teaspoons cayenne pepper
1 1/4 teaspoons dried oregano
1 teaspoon ground black pepper
3 teaspoons corn starch

PUMPKIN PIE SPICE

2 teaspoons ground ginger
3 tablespoons ground cinnamon
1 1/2 teaspoons allspice
1 teaspoon ground clove
1 1/2 teaspoons ground nutmeg

MRS. DASH-INSPIRED SALT-FREE SEASONING

1/4 cup onion flakes
1/4 cup dehydrated sweet pepper flakes
1 tablespoon garlic powder
1 teaspoon basil
1 teaspoon parsley
1 teaspoon oregano
1 teaspoon thyme
1/2 teaspoon cumin
1/2 teaspoon coriander
1/2 teaspoon dry mustard
1/4 teaspoon celery seed
1 tablespoon dehydrated lemon zest
2 teaspoons black pepper

SLOPPY JOE MIX

1 teaspoon salt
1 tablespoon brown sugar
2 teaspoons chili powder
1 tablespoon dry mustard
1 1/2 tablespoons onion flakes
1 tablespoon smoked paprika
2 tablespoons dehydrated sweet pepper (optional)
1 teaspoon ground cumin
1 1/2 teaspoons garlic powder
1 teaspoon black pepper

To make: Add this mix to 1 can of tomato sauce, 2 tablespoons vinegar, 1 diced sweet pepper, and 1 pound meatless crumbles.

GAZPACHO

PAGE 26

RESOURCES

HappyCow.net will help you find nearby plant-based vegan food wherever you are.

RETAIL CHEESE ALTERNATIVES

Please read the ingredients carefully, as not all products are vegan-friendly.

Daiya Foods
daiyafoods.com

Follow Your Heart
followyourheart.com

Go Veggie
goveggiefoods.com/vegan

Kite Hill
kite-hill.com

Miyoko's Kitchen
miyokoskitchen.com

Pure Abundance Artisan Vegan Cheese
pureabundancefood.com

MILK ALTERNATIVES

Please read the ingredients carefully, as not all products are vegan-friendly.

Almond Breeze
almondbreeze.com

Califia Farms
califiafarms.com

Pacific Foods
pacificfoods.com

Silk
silk.com/soymilk

Simple Truth
simpletruth.com

So Delicious
sodeliciousdairyfree.com

Tempt
livingharvest.com

WestSoy
westsoymilk.com

MEAT ALTERNATIVES

Please read the ingredients carefully, as not all products are vegan-friendly.

Boca
bocaburger.com

Beyond Meat
beyondmeat.com

Field Roast
fieldroast.com

Gardein
gardein.com

Lightlife
lightlife.com

No Evil Foods
noevilfoods.com

Simple Truth
simpletruth.com

EGG REPLACEMENTS (FOR BAKING)

For each egg in a baking recipe, you can substitute:

Applesauce
1/3 cup applesauce

Aquafaba
3 tablespoons, whisked until frothy

Baking Soda & Vinegar
1 teaspoon baking soda + 1 tablespoon white vinegar

Banana
1/4 cup ripe, mashed banana

Flax
1 tablespoon ground flax + 3 tablespoons water

SUMMER PASTA SALAD

PAGE 39

NOTES

NOTES

NOTES

THANK YOU

This book would not have been possible without the generous support of many people, including my amazing Kickstarter support team:

Hope Capps
Carolina McVeagh
Dougal Campbell
Kaisa
Kimberly Milam
Michael McKinley
Rhonda Fleming Hayes
Robyn Doig
Kim Brown
Eric Roux
Jhim Midgett
Beth Skony
Heidi Berry
Erika Sturgies
Jason Lye
Darrin Johns
Deaf_tone_mushroom
Tiffany Marcheterre
Kala Turner
"Farmer Tyler" Baras
Steve Lavoie
Joleen Nichols
Bob Covey
James Burke
Drake Collins
Ann Lang
Rhonda Newsome
Christopher Ruggeri
LesleyDawn Robertson
Amy Stanley
Susan Richmond
Desiree White

Justin Matlock
Jen Foley
Briget McManus
Norman
Russell Bowman
Nathan Strange
Douglas Cooper-Fleming
Tina Tait
Brian Dowd
Sunshine Steiner
Ilona Kersey
Nina Catanese
Katie Pope
Brinna Durney
Shawna Coronado
Buffy Chapman
Mary Callahan
Miriam Goldberger
Ernest Allred
Rebecca Pruett
Mia Nichols
Sharon Bussey-Reschka
Sterling Woodward
Sharon Sturm
Kylee Baumle
Julie Adolf
Mark Brenner
Andy Seabolt
Michelle Biddix-Simmons
Sagdrina Jalal
Jill Fazio

Stig-Jørund B. Arnesen
Maria Pinkleton
Kenny Point
Katie Elzer-Peters
Fae Donegan
77Christine Hurray
Justin P. Moore
Sally
Heather Melton
Holly Christine Brown
Beth Kelley
Noreen Devchand
Amy Chiabotta
Denise Koch
Jen Neve
Chris Alnutt
Mia Graves
Shondra
Tod Champion
Stephen Jones
Melanie Teegarden
Rachael Bazzett
Dawn Kelly
Alyssa Windley
Frank Anderson
James Moore
John Justen
Moe Loughran
Jenny Nybro Peterson
Jodi Wenz
Claire Culbreth
Fred Yelk Woodruff

INDEX

BETTER THAN BUTTERMILK BISCUITS

PAGE 20

Made in the USA
Columbia, SC
22 May 2017